Wildlife as Property Owners

Wildlife as Property Owners

A New Conception of Animal Rights

KAREN BRADSHAW

The University of Chicago Press ❋ *Chicago and London*

The University of Chicago Press, Chicago 60637
The University of Chicago Press, Ltd., London
© 2020 by The University of Chicago
Published 2020
Printed in the United States of America

29 28 27 26 25 24 23   2 3 4 5

ISBN-13: 978-0-226-57122-5 (cloth)
ISBN-13: 978-0-226-57136-2 (paper)
ISBN-13: 978-0-226-57153-9 (e-book)
DOI: https://doi.org/10.7208
/chicago/9780226571539.001.0001

Library of Congress Cataloging-in-Publication Data

Names: Bradshaw, Karen, author.
Title: Wildlife as property owners : a new conception of
    animal rights / Karen Bradshaw.
Description: Chicago : University of Chicago Press, 2020. |
    Includes bibliographical references and index.
Identifiers: LCCN 2020019260 | ISBN 9780226571225 (cloth) |
    ISBN 9780226571362 (paperback) |
    ISBN 9780226571539 (ebook)
Subjects: LCSH: Animal rights—United States. |
    Rights of nature—United States. | Right of property—
    United States. | Land tenure—United States. |
    Human-animal relationships—United States. |
    Animals—Law and legislation—United States. |
    Animal diversity—United States. | Nature—
    Effect of human beings on.
Classification: LCC KF3841 .B73 2020 | DDC 346.7304—dc23
LC record available at https://lccn.loc.gov/2020019260

For Camellia

Contents

Introduction

Humankind coexists with all other living things. People drink the same water, breathe the same air, and share the same land as other animals. Yet property law reflects a general assumption that only people can own land. The effects of this presumption are disastrous for wildlife and humans alike. Anthropocentric property is a key driver of biodiversity loss, a silent killer of species worldwide. Biodiversity loss is the greatest environmental challenge of our time, surpassing climate change in urgency and importance. The linchpin of conserving wildlife is identifying the effects of the legal fiction that only people can own property. If excluding animals from a legal right to own land is causing their destruction, extending the legal right to own property to wildlife may prove its salvation. This book advocates for folding animals into our existing system of property law, giving them the option to own land just as humans do.

The Problem of Biodiversity Loss

The alarm bells ringing about biodiversity loss are growing louder. We are on the precipice of massive extinction, caused by human action. If we believe leading scientists' urgent warnings, designating land for animals is not only crucial for protecting wildlife—it is equally vital for the survival of humankind. The only viable solution is setting aside habitat for wildlife.

In 2015, Elizabeth Kolbert's best-selling book *The Sixth Extinction: An Unnatural History* introduced a mainstream American audience to looming, catastrophic biodiversity loss.[1] Kolbert meticulously interwove the tales of thirteen species with a comprehensive analysis of the historical and present state of scientific thinking. She brought warnings previously confined to scholarly conversation to the American public.

Mainstream Americans are beginning to focus on biodiversity loss: At what point is it too much? How many species can be lost before trophic cascade occurs, where entire food chains or ecosystems collapse because key species are removed from the system? Absent conscientious and coordinated action, many species will become extinct. Habitat loss is endemic and worsening. By some accounts, only a massive designation of land as habitat for animals can prevent widespread extinctions.

Last year, famed biologist E. O. Wilson proposed setting aside half of the land on earth for animals in order to avoid catastrophic species loss. "Unless humanity learns a great deal more about global diversity and moves quickly to protect it, we will soon lose most of the species comprising life on earth."[2] Wilson argues that we must not forget our survival depends on other living things. He advocates for dedicating specific lands to promote wildlife survival. Although he did an artful job of framing the benefits of his proposal, Wilson did not outline the vital legal or institutional questions that his bold vision required.

This book provides that missing link: a legal framework to propose how one could actually respond to the problem that Kolbert highlights and the solution that Wilson offers. For decades, scholars have noted that land development leads to habitat loss, which drives biodiversity loss. I link these observations with property law concepts to develop real-world solutions to habitat conservation.

The Proposal: Fold Wildlife into Existing Property Law

This book charts a novel legal avenue through which property law can give life to wildlife interests and rights of nature. Property law is a stolid, well-developed body of law that has ploddingly developed over centuries with a steady focus on stability. It also happens to be the backbone of capitalism. Rather than focus conservation efforts solely on expanding environmental laws, I suggest, perhaps we should integrate nature into the current system of property. To be clear, I am not advocating for humans to own wildlife as property (an argument others make), I am arguing for something far more radical, an interspecies system of property.

My argument is very simple. The law should allow animals to own land, just as you and I can. Animals would own land through a trust, managed by a human trustee. A "trust" is a legal instrument managed by one person (a "trustee") for the benefit of others (the "beneficiaries"). Trustees have a fiduciary duty to act in the best interests of the beneficiaries rather than in their own. The trust is an existing, widely used tool. Millions of Americans already use trusts to manage their homes and assets.

Under my proposal to protect biodiversity, human trustees would manage land for animal beneficiaries at an ecosystem level.[3] Trustees would weigh the competing interests of wildlife constituencies within the ecosystem. A mix of public and private oversight would protect against possible abuse of this system. Judges would evaluate whether trustees are acting in the best interest of animal beneficiaries, just as they do for any other beneficiaries.

Expanding property rights to a previously excluded group does not change the existing framework of property. Existing land ownership, property boundaries, rights to exclude animals, and systems of recording property remain totally unchanged under my proposal. Rights expansion is not redistribution; no one takes land or property away from current landowners. Wildlife that earn rights do not get a windfall of free land. Instead, the possibility of future transactions just expands. Instead of selling your land to another person, you could choose to sell it to an animal-owned trust instead.

My proposed interspecies system of property does not displace existing environmental laws or fundamentally alter property law.

The Urgency of Action

There has never been a time more important for legal thinkers to reimagine how to reconcile humankind and nature. People increasingly understand that biodiversity is crucial to the fate of our species and continued planetary survival. Saving wildlife is analogous to saving the planet. The crisis of unprecedent species extinction demands our attention. Judges, lawyers, activists, scholars, students must act boldly and wisely to transform public concern into pragmatic, effective solutions.

My proposal primarily focuses on wildlife. It does not serve to free chimpanzees from cages or free cattle destined for slaughter. My proposal does not even suggest that wildlife would become substantial, or even equal, property owners. No landowner loses their property or is required to host wildlife. It merely aligns law with existing social mores regarding the treatment of animals.

My objective in proposing property rights for animals complements, but differs from, the goals of many animal rights groups. For example, organizations such as the People for the Ethical Treatment of Animals (PETA) and the Nonhuman Rights Project are seeking legal personhood and a degree of human rights for some animals, particularly for creatures like whales, dolphins, monkeys, and chimpanzees. These organizations include policies such as banning medical testing on primates and confining orcas in tanks.

My proposal is distinct. I am proposing a limited category of property rights—the kind of rights that law has long afforded to ships, corporations, children, and the mentally incapacitated.

Under my conception, wildlife has the land it needs, but people can still eat a burger or swat a mosquito.

The problem of biodiversity loss is clear. The solution of preserving land for animals is straightforward. Leaders exist who are ready to take action for wildlife. What has been missing thus far is the legal pathway, a roadmap of how to preserve vital biodiversity within our existing legal institutions.

Overview of the Book

Chapter 1, *The Nexus of Animal Rights and the Rights of Nature*, provides a literature review. I identify the proposal in this book as sitting at the nexus of animal law, the rights of nature literature within environmental law, and property law. First, I explain animal law as fundamentally divided into competing "welfare" and "rights" approaches. Second, I explain the rights of nature literature, which considers granting rights to a broader spectrum of living things. Third, I turn to property law and begin a quick primer on its relevant features. Nonlawyers should note that property law is distinctive from other substantive areas of law (such as environmental law) in ways that are crucial to evaluating the proposal. Then, I outline a key question in property law that relates to this project: how property rights emerge. Finally, I flag a few key scientific and philosophical literatures that address animal behavior with respect to land, how humans can determine what animals want, and a political theory of animal rights, including property rights.

Chapter 2, *Biodiversity Loss as a Property Law Problem*, argues that human land uses are the leading source of habitat loss; habitat loss is the leading cause of species extinction. Preserving wildlife requires preserving habitat, which means leaving land undeveloped. The Western European tradition unthinkingly assumes that animals cannot own land. As a result, we have failed to see the powerful property-based solutions to biodiversity loss.

Chapter 3, *The Biological Origins of Property*, makes the novel claim that an interspecies system of property already exists.

Reviewing animal behavior shows that the core tenets of how one comes to own and defend space are remarkably consistent among species. This includes species on every limb of the so-called tree of life, such as ants and bees. I provide specific examples of animal behavior that mirror the central features of property law.

Chapter 4, *Uncovering Animal Rights in Existing Property Law*, argues that animal ownership of property is not hypothetical. Animals have strong property interests in the United States today. We have simply failed to understand them as such. This chapter demonstrates that animal property rights are both woven into the very foundations of our system of property and scattered throughout it. It discusses customary and common-law rights. Many precolonial indigenous legal systems envisioned animals as coequal rights-holders to land. (The notion that Native Americans did not have systems of property is a pervasive myth that colonists used to expropriate land from indigenous peoples.) Colonial courts and legislatures could not conceive of animals as rights-holders and thus never extinguished their interests in land. Precolonial property interests are dormant, not dead, if they were not explicitly extinguished. Additionally, Congress has enacted dozens of pieces of legislation granting animals an extensive web of property-based rights embedded in many different statutes. Creating rights for animals to occupy space is not revolutionary. If anything, eliminating existing animal interests would be the more radical act.

Chapter 5, *Using Legal Trusts to Implement a System of Animal Property Rights*, overviews the nuts-and-bolts of how animals can own property. It sketches the basic model of animal-owned trusts managed by human trustees at an ecosystem level. It addresses the crucial issue of how humans might discern animal interests and offers a glimpse into the institutional mechanisms that might facilitate this process.

Chapter 6, *Traditional Legal Pathways to Formalizing Animal Property Rights*, outlines the statutory and litigation-based pathways to animal property rights. It provides the roadmap of how wildlife advocates can extend, formalize, and leverage existing animal property rights for the sake of biodiversity protection. Through legal processes, advocates for animals can ask legislators and judges to establish the boundaries of animal property rights.

Chapter 7, *Leveraging Property Rights to Aid Biodiversity*, leverages the creativity of property law to craft a bottom-up, crowdsourced approach to animal property ownership. It highlights things that wildlife advocates can do today to actualize the property-based gains in land and beyond. This chapter shows how nongovernmental organizations, individuals, corporations, and states can leverage their assets to benefit wildlife through immediate private action.

Chapter 8, *Case Studies of Stakeholder Collaborations Managing Resource Competition between Humans and Wildlife*, provides three case studies of people navigating wildlife interests in land and resources. Case study 1 considers competition between wild horses and cattle ranchers for forage on public lands. Case study 2 tells the story of the United States funding thick-billed parrot recovery in Mexico instead of restoring the bird population domestically. Case study 3 focuses on a stakeholder collaboration managing a caribou herd in Alaska. Collectively, lessons from these collaborations show the role of people in managing wildlife.

Chapter 9, *Evaluating a Property-Based Approach to Biodiversity Preservation*, notes that the key benefit of expanding animals' property ownership is the long-term preservation of habitat. Animals presently have limited bargaining power with respect to land. This proposal gives them access to the market and places a dollar value on where they live. The fiduciary duties of trustees would work in tandem with the standards of the private governing body to ensure that animals could not be stripped of their habitat. This move would serve to assign value to animal habitat and entrust that habitat for animal protection. It would remove species' well-being from the political whims of Congress and empower individual wildlife enthusiasts to preserve habitat in a more permanent way. Further, this would allow more accurate quantitative national assessments of the amount, value, and locations of animal habitats, which could lead to better preservation and management decisions.

Chapter 10, *The Implications of Interspecies Ownership on Property Theory*, considers how the observations in this book may affect legal scholars' conception of how property emerges.

The conclusion considers the implications for a property approach to the rights of nature—giving all living things (plants, bacteria, ecosystems) the status of rights-holders vested at an ecosystem level. I briefly consider the arguments developed earlier for animal property interests as applied to all living things. This analysis reveals that the arguments used to advance animal property ownership apply equally to ecosystem property rights. Just as Congress has created rights for animals to own land, so too has it created existence and property rights for plants and waterways. Just as indigenous governments have—and do—create legal rights for animals, so too do they extend rights to other living things. Perhaps most surprisingly, just as animals allocate and compete for territorial space in a manner that mirrors human property behavior, so too do plants, bacteria, and ecosystems. For these reasons, I conclude that the appropriate framing of expanding property interests likely will extend beyond wildlife to ecosystems or nature more broadly.

Part I

A Foundational Understanding of Animal Property Law

The Nexus of Animal Rights and the Rights of Nature

Property-based solutions to biodiversity loss sit at the nexus of three legal literatures: animal law, environmental law, and property law. Philosophers and scientists have also considered the questions at the heart of my proposal, particularly with respect to human obligations to wildlife. This chapter briefly reviews the relevant literatures.

Animals and the Law

Animal law scholars are sharply divided between the welfare approach and the rights approach. Until roughly fifty years ago, animal law focused on improving the treatment of animals within their present social conditions (a welfare approach). Then, Peter Singer, Tom Regan, and Gary Francione began the animal rights movement, advocating for change in the legal status of animals. The ideological debate between welfarists and rights advocates has dominated the scholarly conversation in the field for nearly fifty years. Perhaps because of this binary focus, legal innovations have not kept pace with rapidly changing social attitudes toward animals. Most notably, existing approaches to animal law focus on animals in captivity and have largely overlooked wildlife interests.

Animal welfare focuses on helping animals physically and mentally cope with their surrounding conditions. Modern welfarists focus on pragmatic, instrumentalist lobbying, and litigation to improve animals' lives. Welfarists' goals can be quite diverse and include aims like criminalizing dogfighting, reducing market opportunities for "puppy mills" with inhumane breeding conditions, and preventing cruel factory farm conditions. Many people are familiar with the work of Temple Grandin, whose focus on better systems for handling, transporting, and handling livestock is a classic welfarist approach.

Economic arguments for welfarism suggest human owners of animals are incentivized to invest in proper care for their animals because it is in their own interest to do so. Judge Richard Posner articulates this position, saying: "One way to protect animals is to make them property because people tend to protect what they own."[1]

Most of existing animal law reflects a welfare approach. A mix of local, state, and federal legislation serves to prevent socially unacceptable treatment of animals. For example, the federal Animal Welfare Act, an anticruelty statute, is designed as a backstop to prevent egregious cruelty or abuse.

Critics like animal advocate Tom Regan have argued that the welfare approach insufficiently protects in practice and is both theoretically and morally wanting. For example, the Animal Welfare Act excludes from protection farm animals, birds, rats, and mice.[2] Similarly, the Bald and Golden Eagle Protection Act, Wild Free-Roaming Horses and Burros Act, the Marine Mammal Protection Act, and Endangered Species Act are limited to only some animals. Further, few existing statutes grant animals standing to sue for the enforcement of rights, leading to underenforcement since activists do not have a legal basis to bring a claim on their behalf.

In the 1970s, animal rights theory emerged as an alternative to the welfare approach. Advocates designed the rights-based model to radically reshape human-animal relationships by dramatically extending legal protections for animals. Today, animal rights efforts focus on establishing legal personhood and some associated rights for animals.

Animal rights theory suggests some animals possess sufficiently human-like characteristics that it is immoral to kill them for use as food or fur or to keep them in captivity. Peter Singer famously argued that all beings who are capable of suffering should be considered equally for humane treatment. Tom Regan suggests that mammals possess consciousness and thus have an identity that vests them with inherent value. He takes a stronger stance than Singer, suggesting that people should not use mammals for food, testing, or research. Regan captures the distinction between animal welfare and animal rights theory, saying: "Not for larger cages, we declare, empty cages."[3]

Several legal theorists have contributed to the growing rights literature. Professor Gary Francione has devoted his career as a legal scholar to advancing a strong articulation of the rights approach, criticizing welfarists as insufficiently protecting animal interests. "The rights theorist rejects the use of animals in experiments, or for human consumption, because such use violates fundamental obligations of *justice* that humans owe to nonhumans, and not simply because these activities cause animals to suffer."[4]

Professor David Farve focuses on considering the role of animal interests in the legal system, past and present. He advocates for balancing human and animal interests in various contexts.[5] Professor Justin Marceau's recently published book, *Beyond Cages: Animal Law and Criminal Punishment*, considers welfarists' calls for greater criminalization of animal abuses against the harms of mass incarceration, highlighting the hypocrisy of "carceral animal law."[6] Cass Sunstein and Laurence Tribe have written about animal standing, the issue of whether courts can adjudicate claims brought by (or on behalf of) animals.[7]

Attorney Steven Wise, the founder of the Nonhuman Rights Project, has spearheaded a sophisticated, multidecade litigation strategy arguing that animals have certain constitutional rights. The animals-as-legal-persons model for which Wise advocates represents a bold and novel vision. It has captured public attention. However, some judicial commentators criticize this approach as having no broadly socially acceptable end. A campaign that may someday succeed tremendously has thus far experienced only moderate success in courts.

Although animal rights theorists are doing important work on numerous fronts, the current approach is at once overly and insufficiently broad. Judges forecasting the logical endpoint of existing positions see veganism and the end of domestic animals, which have led them to resist more moderate points and to raise concerns of a slippery slope. And the approach fails to capture many animals worthy of protection, including wildlife and sea creatures. It does little to limit habitat destruction due to land development, the leading cause of wildlife loss. Moreover, many theorists focus on creatures higher on the so-called tree of life, that is, creatures that are sufficiently human-like.

This distinction encapsulates a human-centric basis for protection that some find problematic. It also overlooks creatures, like ants and bees, which maintain remarkably sophisticated social systems but fail to evidence the demonstrations of intelligence used to justify the improved treatment of elephants, whales, and chimpanzees.

The reliance on animals' cognitive similarities to humans to justify rights produces distributional effects in the animal kingdom. Chimpanzees may be afforded rights based on their human-like qualities, but ants would not. This dichotomization of species suggests that investment of energy in the nonhuman rights movement as currently crafted helps primates but diverts resources from many more species. The counterargument, of course, is that affording human rights to chimpanzees is the first step in a long journey toward more expansive rights for all animals. But, by forecasting its eventual goal, the human rights movement seemingly sabotages its success by creating judicial and scholarly reticence based on eventual outcome.

Although environmental law and natural resources law schol- ars have long studied wildlife, they have only recently begun situating wildlife concerns in the animal law conversation. Pro- fessors Irus Baverman and Annecoos Wiersema are doing im- portant work highlighting wildlife considerations, particularly against the backdrop of climate change.[8] In a three-part book series, Baverman has traced the role of zoos and other nongov- ernmental organizations in keeping species from extinction. Wi- ersema focuses on the global challenges of conservation, a particu- larly vital aspect for many species. Their efforts highlight that human effects on wildlife are mostly unwitnessed: slow-moving and difficult to trace to a specific cause on a case-by-case basis. For these reasons, the comparative suffering of wildlife is likely underappreciated relative to the most vivid cases.

Ecosystems theory has permeated virtually every other realm of public consciousness. We generally understand that every creature in a system is dependent on other creatures in the shared natural environment; yet the habitat needs of wildlife are largely a blind spot within the animal rights movement until recently. The work of Baverman and Wiersema show that the limitations of focusing more on animals than their habitat is producing per- verse results. Some animals "saved" from extinction exist only in captivity, their natural habitat permanently destroyed. There is no place in the wild to which they can return. Lions are bred and kept in captivity in Africa, released only for safari hunters to kill them. Similarly, trophy hunting for African animals living in captivity in Texas is now a billion-dollar industry, justified as a conservation effort.

The law on the books is out of step with public sentiment for the treatment of animals. In 2001, fewer than one dozen law schools in the United States offered an animal law course. Today, over 150 do. Several top law schools have opened clin- ics and centers devoted to animal law. Students and donors are demanding that law schools hire full-time, tenure-track faculty who will boldly innovate. It appears that the field of animal law is at a much-needed inflection point, where a multitude of new approaches will flood the space long dominated by the welfare-versus-rights debate.

My property-based solution to biodiversity loss will not unilaterally unwind the decades-long feud between welfare and rights approaches to animal law. Adding a new, alternative approach may, however, breathe new life into a field that has become focused on a single debate without considering the plethora of other avenues to achieve the overarching goal: better treatment of animals. This book's present limitation to wildlife and domestic pets adds fuel to the fire of new ideas, showing how the ongoing welfare versus rights debate has short-changed a large segment of the worldwide animal population by focusing scholarly attention on too narrow a set of questions.

Rights of Nature

In 1972, environmental law scholar Christopher Stone considered the legal questions associated with granting rights to living things that are not human in *Do Trees Have Standing? Towards Legal Rights for Natural Objects*. Stone said he was "quite seriously proposing that we give legal rights to forests, oceans, rivers, and other so-called 'natural objects' in the environment—indeed to the natural environment as a whole."[9] A pragmatist, Stone quickly addressed the key arguments against the legal extension of rights to nature, noting: "Now, to say that the natural environment should have rights is not to say anything as silly as that no one should cut down a tree."

Stone's focus was on legal personhood, the standing to sue in court to obtain judicial relief. This differs slightly from property rights, but it nevertheless overlaps in meaningful ways. For reasons that may not be clear to nonlawyers, property rights are distinct from other rights. For a crude and strictly descriptive comparison to make this point, consider that a person may own property but also be legally confined in prison or even executed by the government. On the other hand, an entity that can own property can sue to enforce the rights a property owner enjoys.

In this way, animals who own property can achieve Stone's goal of the right to sue. For example, it is legal for a pet to inherit a home through a trust in most American states today. There is no question the trustee could sue to enforce property-related claims, such as an action against a trespasser against the land. In this way, property law could be used—and is being used—to create de facto standing for animals to sue.

Stone's paper noted that legal rights had, over time, been extended to groups of people once considered ineligible for such rights. Stone further noted that nonhumans have also been recognized as possessors of rights, including: "trusts, corporations, joint ventures, municipalities, Subchapter R partnerships, . . . national-states," and ships.

Stone noted that natural objects were ineligible for three forms of rights: (1) standing, (2) damages, and (3) beneficiaries of awards. Since then, the influential Ninth Circuit Court of Appeals has allowed people to bring cases on behalf of animals in the animals' names. Further, municipalities and indigenous governments in the United States have granted natural objects legal personhood. Concerning the second and third rights, Congress has created several statutory remedies—all under the broader umbrella of natural resources damages—which allow the government to collect damages for certain kinds of harms to wildlife or wildlife habitat, the proceeds of which can only be used to benefit animals. In this sense, there is a tentative realization of Stone's goal.

A decade ago, giving nature property rights was a radical thought experiment. Today it is a burgeoning movement, internationally and within the United States. Brazil and Ecuador have included a human right to nature in their constitution.[10] New Zealand gave a river the legal status of persons. Australia granted a river a right to nature. People have granted Lake Erie legal personhood. The Yurok Tribe in California declared legal personhood for the Klamath River; several tribal constitutions within the United States include rights for nature. Indigenous peoples worldwide are forerunners of this movement, coordinating with one another to grant rights to natural objects. The world is paying attention; legal scholars have been slower to note how existing courts and institutions might interpret these rights.

Meanwhile, scholars have made considerable efforts to consider animal perspectives.[11] Dozens of law review articles in the United States have discussed the rights of nature. David R. Boyd has published *The Rights of Nature*, a book documenting instances of the movement. Swedish ecologist Guillaume Chapron led a team of authors in publishing an article in *Science*, a leading scientific journal, considering rights of nature. In 2019, a group of professors met to discuss how, and whether, to integrate rights of nature within the European Union. Amid this growing scholarly attention, envisioning ecosystem ownership of land provides a new pathway within this popular but still-nascent literature.

Property Law

Property law is both a robust academic field and an area of legal practice. It describes how things come to be owned, maintained, and transferred. Property is very different from other substantive bodies of law with which nonlawyers might be familiar. Although the field is far too expansive to survey here, I briefly sketch a few key features of property law that make it a particularly interesting path for approaching questions of biodiversity. The key features of property to understand are its common-law nature, neutrality as among owners, stability, and ability and incentive to innovate.

Unlike many other areas of law, property law is based on common law (or judge-made law) as oppose to statutes enacted by the legislature. Courts decide property cases based on precedent, or lines of previously established cases, rather than statutes (which are laws enacted by Congress). Many current property issues are governed by doctrines established by very old cases. English colonists transported English common law to the United States (as did French, Spanish, and Russian colonists), which in turn reflected an uninterrupted lineage from older European systems.

Property law contains the rules for accumulating and transferring wealth through belongings. It does not discriminate as between owners—if someone can own property, they are subject to all of the same rules and obligations as other property owners. With respect to animals, this creates a protective effect by casting the lot of all property owners together. Disparate interests are intertwined through property.

The rights of nonhumans to participate in property are well established. Corporations and trusts are human-created legal instruments that extend beyond the human lifespan, yet are co-equal participants in our system of property. For centuries, courts have allowed people who are incapacitated or unable to represent themselves to own property, represented by trusted third parties. Tools including trust law and fiduciary duties are widely used and well understood by mainstream attorneys.

For centuries, legal institutions have crafted and refined standards and procedural processes to help guide people deciding the best interests of others, even when those interests are unknowable. Legal concepts like fiduciary duties, custodianship, and trust law serve to protect the interests of persons and things not able to meaningfully advocate for themselves. These are robust areas of law which could seamlessly accommodate animal interests.

Property law is remarkably stable. There is a well-established, widely followed system of land titling and recordation. In general, there are rules, people follow them, courts make decisions, law enforcement officials carry out the orders of a court. Land is divided, boundaries are recorded, once recorded they can only change through a subsequent recording. Property transfers according to preset default rules. Intellectual property—like copyrights and patents—also operates through similarly stable systems.

A unique feature of property is that the government may not take it away without paying for it. If Congress grants animals a legislative protection, a later Congress may reverse that protection. (The same authority is given presidents, agencies, governors, and judges.) So, even hard-fought legal battles to protect animals might be diminished or reversed in the future. Property, however, has a permanence. The Fifth Amendment of the Constitution—known as the Takings Clause—provides: "No person shall . . . be deprived of life, liberty, or property, without due process of law; nor shall private property be taken for public use, without just compensation." ("Person" is legal person.) Property rights are expansive and extend beyond land. For example, patents and copyrights are considered intellectual property.

For centuries, legal scholars and economists have considered how one comes to own. Leading historical scholars like John Locke, Adam Smith, and William Blackstone advanced varying theories for how private property rights emerge.[12] Yet modern scholars agree that central question remains unanswered: How *do* private property rights emerge?[13] When do they recede? These questions are fundamentally correlated to the most pressing property debates of our time: whether markets drive property rights; whether property is defined by exclusion or inclusion; and whether property is better held privately or communally.

In 1967, Harold Demsetz provided a law and economics account for the conditions under which property rights emerge. Demsetz theorized that when "the gains of internalization become larger than the cost of internalization" rights will emerge.[14] He compared the systems of property maintained by Native Americans of the southwest plains and those of the Labrador peninsula—two regions with markedly different physical geographies. Demsetz noted that the Native Americans of the southwest plains did not have private property rights for two reasons: first, because there were no plains animals with a high market value, and second because the animals on the landscapes were primarily grazing species who wandered over large areas. Under such conditions, it was not worthwhile for the Native Americans in the region to privatize land. In the Labrador peninsula during the fur trading period, however, beavers had a high commercial value and small territories. As a result, the cost of internalizing the maintenance of private hunting lands was justified—causing Native Americans to protect family territories.

Demsetz's cost-based formulation became the starting point for ongoing inquiry into the emergence of rights.[15] In 2002, Tom Merrill rephrased Demsetz's core notion as: "property rights emerge when the social benefits of establishing such rights exceed their social costs." Merrill summarized Demsetz's arguments in three points: First, a system of private property encourages resource development relative to an open-access common. Second, private property reduces rent dissipation relative to open-access regimes. And third, the existence of property creates a smaller group of people who must coordinate to control spillover effects. Merrill flagged the open question of the field as:

> [W]e need a theory as to when and why private-exclusion rights emerge, and ideally this theory would explain the rise and fall of exclusion rights, not the rise and fall of any and all organized efforts to "internalize externalities."[16]

Since that workshop, scholars have continued the discussion of the emergence of property rights.

Two of the leading debates within property law relate to this question. First, the dividing line between modern property theorists revolves around the linchpin of exclusionary[17] or inclusive[18] approaches. This is not a matter of description; the framing leads to the normative concern about the progressiveness of property, the extent to which it is communal, and the desirability of social inputs on "private" rights.

Second, many modern property law scholars have focused on the human institutions surrounding property—the state, government, contract, markets. Yet, reams of literature on the emergence of rights have discounted the biological features of property rights. This exists in tension with an increasing number of observations suggesting that property is separable from formal, legal institutions. At a further degree of abstraction, property as reliant on government (or not) relates to the normative question of the appropriate degree of government involvement in property, long a central theme among libertarian scholars.

In sum, two of the leading debates in property law (and law more generally) relate to the yet-unanswered questions about how rights emerge, persist, and dissipate. In my view, the latter informs the former, at least partially. The leading property theories do link the emergence of property rights to the natural world—the physical space in which the rights emerge. Yet, the underlying geophysical and ecological conditions play a vital, unaccounted role in describing when rights emerge and dissipate. Below, I outline how some scholars have overcome that limitation. In fact, I argue that their work represents a growing paradigm shift away from well-studied human institutions and toward lesser-considered biological factors, a shift that may influence the broader scholarly analysis of property rights.

The New, Biological Paradigm

An alternative, biological account of how property rights emerged now exists—although it has not yet been fully recognized as such. This account is premised on a long-standing yet under-appreciated line of property scholarship. Embedded in generations of work by leading theorists, I suggest, rests a yet-inchoate paradigm for approaching the question of how rights emerge. Collectively, this body of work considers the biological inputs into the existence and content of property rights, rules, and laws.

Although Western property theorists have long assumed that only humans had property rights,[19] they also noted the natural, universal nature of rights. Plato described law as operating in accordance with nature.[20] Aristotle described law as "universal" and "all-embracing."[21] John Locke described property as a "natural right" that preexisted government.[22] Blackstone believed that human property behavior operated along principles reducible to mathematical equations.[23] Natural law scholars believed that it was useful to look at human behavior divorced from government, but ended at the human—not considering broader biological principles.

Leading thinkers of our time have more directly questioned the biological underpinnings of property beyond mankind, beginning with mere footnotes and sentences by scholars. Ronald Coase noted that various restrictions on property use do "not come about simply because of Government regulation" and "would be true under any system of law."[24] In 1978, David Hume suggested that natural law may have emerged from our species, or any.[25] Henry Smith noted that the custom of deferring to the possessors of property is "very widespread" including "all of society or close to it."[26] Richard Epstein noted that property statutes "do not resemble in the slightest conscious social planning."[27] Piecing these disparate references together suggests a widespread view that all humans, or perhaps even all animals, operate under similar property principles.

Eventually, this became quite direct, with a leading scholar making side-by-side comparisons of human and animal behavior. In 1993 Robert Ellickson devoted a single sentence to animals as maintaining usufructary interests, and he briefly discussed animal treatment of property in brief references and footnotes found in other work.[28] Ellickson also briefly acknowledged the parallel between human and animal boundary marking, noting that some species use sounds and smells to assert territorial claims and that dogs "are superb boundary defenders" of human property.[29] In 2011, Ellickson briefly noted that bird species used sound to establish property. Tantalizingly, Ellickson equated "claim[ing] property" with "assert[ing] a territorial claim" but did not expand on this parallel.[30]

Eventually, scholars broke further ground on this subject. In 1999, Richard Pipes devoted three pages to discussing territorial possessiveness among animals in a book on property law.[31] In 2004, Jeffrey Evans Stake spent several paragraphs exploring how intergenerational property transfer rules for humans and animals alike might suggest "ancient biological antecedents" and outlining parallels between animal territoriality and human behavior with respect to inheritance.[32]

The largest breakthrough occurred in 2009, when the influential property scholar and casebook author James Krier published *Evolutionary Theory and the Origin of Property Rights*.[33] In it, Krier provided a thorough, careful treatment of the implications of a game theoretical model based on animal territoriality but applied to human behavior.[34] This contribution built on the biologists John Maynard Smith and Geoff A. Parker's 1976 frame-work for evolutionarily stable strategy models of animal behav-ior, using a hawk/dove analysis to demonstrate that animals that could assess the likelihood of winning physical contests with their rivals, and then assess the merit of actually engaging in such conflict, would be favored by evolutionary selection.[35]

Krier's innovation rested not in the link between human prop-erty rights and animal territoriality; other scholars had already made that initial leap in biology, economics, law, and biology. [36] Instead, Krier provided a different but important insight: that property law scholars should use models developed in biological studies to inform how property rights emerged among humans.

Krier's influential article has been cited over 110 times in a wide array of interdisciplinary journals, including many articles written by leading property scholars. Despite this attention, it has received less recognition than it is due. The most interesting innovation of Krier's article has been often cited, seldom discussed, and rarely built upon. Only one subsequent law journal article has thus far sought to expand the empirical basis for human biological comparisons.[37] In this sense, and in moving beyond human/animal property rights as a mere matter of curiosity, linking property rights to biology in fact speaks to many of the most fundamental questions in the field.

Three years before Demsetz advanced his well-known theory, Jerram Brown, a leading ornithologist, asked and answered the question: "When should an animal defend a territory?" Brown applied an implicit cost-benefit analysis: suggesting that animals implicitly weigh the harms and benefits of establishing territorial rights. Brown wrote:

> [A] balance must be achieved between the positive values of ac-quired food, mate, nesting area, protection of family, etc., and the negative values of loss of time, energy, and opportunities, and risk of injury. Where this balance may lie in any particular species is influenced by a great variety of factors—to name a few: population density, physiological limitations and susceptibilities of the species, nest construction and site requirements, distance to food from nest, stage of development of young at birth, foraging time necessary to

raise young, clutch size, time necessary to protect young, reaction of potential mate to too much or too little aggressiveness, conspicuousness to predators, migration, climate, weather, size of bird, and richness of food supply.[38]

Animals must expend time and energy to exclude others from their territory. They only do so, Brown posited, when there are not enough resources to readily support all the other animals in the area. Under such conditions of scarcity—too many animals, too few resources—it is worthwhile for animals to defend a defined group of owned resources, to ensure that they have ongoing access to them.

Territoriality exists in a middle zone of resource scarcity and abundance: birds did not defend below a lower limit of food abundance because they could not support their basic energy maintenance costs while defending. Birds also stopped defending territory when food was superabundant, because they did not need to invest defense costs to get the energy they required.[39] In other words, the availability of food, shelter, and sunlight determine the social behavior of animals. This appears to be true across species. Badgers, for example, generally maintain strictly territorial clans during periods of food abundance. During scarcity, however, they transition to solitary, single-sex ranges.[40] Brown related this balance to natural selection, noting that the degree of aggressiveness exhibited by individuals surviving and reproducing offspring would become norms for the population.

Brown was influential—his theory has become well accepted across species. He is credited with helping lay the foundation for sociobiology. Later ornithologists restated Brown's analysis as a bird "will hold a territory when it is 'economically defendable,'" that is, if more or less exclusive use of an area outweighs the costs of its defense.[41] Larger territories create more costs and more benefits.[42] Biologists studying specific animals have refined the mathematical models for specific animals.[43]

Once established, settlements are relatively stable. Migratory birds return to established nesting sites year after year; trout return to the streams in which they were spawned. What legal scholar Lee Fennell might refer to as the *stickiness* of property rights or economists might consider endowment effects exist in nature as well. Thus, the final settlement pattern is, in part, the outcome of trade-offs between (1) the advantages associated with obtaining high-quality territory and the costs of defending it against a site-faithful resident, and (2) the advantages associated with being site faithful and the cost of occupying low-quality territory.[44]

Across species, the original owner of a territory tends to win in contests for that territory. Empirical data gathered across birds, fish, insects, and crustaceans show that residents have greater motivation to fight because they value the resource more.[45] The potential challengers to a territory are framed in cost-benefit terms as well, as when "the usurpation costs would be greater than the acquired benefit."[46]

Under what conditions do territories dissolve? The world's foremost expert on ants, Bert Hölldobler, notes that animals should "dissolve boundaries to allow foraging ranges to overlap." This is the case with honey ants. Studies of beavers similarly show that groups can evolve from individual property ownership to a single-clan range.[47] Animals also appear to like being near neighbors, forming "territorial aggregations." One theory suggests that animals gain larger territories by settling next to previous settlers.[48] Different aspects of territory are more or less defended. Home ranges of individuals may, and do, overlap. This area of overlap is neutral and does not constitute part of the more restricted territory.[49]

While Brown was developing a cost-benefit account of property rights, another ornithologist, Jon Crook, was developing the foundation for another important theory of property behavior. In 1964, Crook challenged existing accounts of socialization as driving animal behavior. Instead, he suggested that animal behavior correlates to the ecological variables of the natural environment. He noted that the "control of population size is . . . considered to be a function of complex interaction between ecological and behavior variables, forming an elaborate 'open system' in which homoeostasis is maintained by direct feed-back between the two classes of variable and not primarily through social regulation alone."[50] In other words, animal behavior interacts with the natural environment in an ever-changing, back-and-forth loop.

Crook suggested that the resource conditions where an animal lives directly impact its social behavior. In essence, Crook proposed that property rights are inexorably intertwined with the underlying resources. Crook and a coauthor later expanded on this thesis, creating an expansive overview of how changed ecological conditions lead to marked behavioral differences among insects, birds, lemurs, and primates.[51] Their conclusions were relatively similar: the availability, topography, and distribution of resources directly influenced animal behavior and society. For example, they find that male aggression is linked to the availability of safe sleeping places—whether, depending on species, there are granite rocks or trees to sleep on markedly changes the male's role. To reemphasize: Where animals live shapes their behavior and social systems.

These articles gave rise to a slew of scholarship showing how differences in ecology caused differences in animal societies. Eventually, scientists linked this concept with a new interest in why animals live in groups. David Macdonald and Dominic Johnson developed an ecological explanation for group living, called the resource distribution hypothesis (RDH).[52]

Groups develop when the smallest economically defensible territory for the basic social unit can also support additional animals. The RDH suggests that the distribution of resources across a landscape can shift the cost-benefit analysis to group living. When "resources are patchily distributed over space and/or time," multiple individuals can share resources, "provided they can all satisfy their resource needs without imposing unsustainable costs on each other."[53] Maintaining a physical space large enough to contain sufficient resource patches to meet requirements may leave excess resources some or all the time.

Today, the RDH is a leading theory among biologists for explaining why animals live in groups. Some scientists suggest that it drives group and social behavior of animals, including social hierarchy and mating patterns.[54] Others believe that RDH causes gigantism among some large animals, such as dinosaurs.[55]

To understand the expansive effects of this hypothesis, consider the chimpanzee and bonobo, primates that are the two closest living relatives to humans. Both chimpanzees and bonobos use gestures, or sign language, to communicate with other members of their species. For example, both wave to greet one another.[56] More than 90 percent of the sign language used by these two species—which live separately and are communicating with conspecies—overlaps. When a bonobo reaches out its hand to touch the mouth of another bonobo, it means, "give it to me"—usually a request for food. When a chimpanzee makes the gesture, it means the same thing. To scientists, these linguistic similarities suggest that both creatures descended from a common ancestor. Although these creatures are genetically quite similar, some of their behaviors are remarkably different. Some trace these differences to the kind of food available at their respective habitats, and, by extension, RDH.[57]

The distribution of food across a landscape also dictates territory size, which translates to social structure. For example, male house mice can define and defend boundaries when food resources are clumped together, which leads to a more rigid social hierarchy.[58] When food is more abundant or of a higher quality within a territory, the mouse will invest more to defend those resources. In other words, animals are highly adapted to the specific features of their physical location.

Biologists also reduce a species decision of whether to manage land collectively to a cost-benefit analysis. RDH is one of several factors that contribute to the cost-benefit analysis of group living. Group hunting, predator defense, and alloparenting may favor group living. Increased infanticide risk, parasitism, or disease might push against it.[59] Communal living emerges when the benefits outweigh the costs; natural selection drives species to engage in a cost-benefit analysis of sociality. It is difficult for scientists to identify the motivation for group living among a species because it may have evolutionarily evolved for one purpose but later adapted to satisfy another purpose under changed conditions.[60]

Discerning What Animals Want

Modern philosophers are doing important work on how people can discern what animals want. In 1974, American philosopher Thomas Nagle considered life from an animal's perspective through the thought experiment of being a bat.[61] Nagel suggested that the bat, as a mammal, has consciousness, but bats are uniquely suited to fly, use echolocation to navigate, and hang upside-down. Given these differences in life experience, Nagel suggests only each individual knows what it is like to be a bat; thus, there exists no such thing as an objective perspective into the life of another because humankind is limited to our own, subjective experience.

Martha Nussbaum, a leading philosopher, applies her capabilities approach to human-animal relationships.[62] She argues that animals have an inherent right to a life well lived, as measured by ten vital characteristics. Nussbaum believes animals' fundamental capabilities mandate that humans afford them certain entitlements, including (1) life; (2) bodily health; (3) bodily integrity; (4) senses, imagination, and thought; (5) emotions; (6) practical reason; (7) affiliation; (8) other species; (9) play; and (10) control over their environment. In a series of ground-breaking writings that have unfolded over decades, Nussbaum explores the promise and limitations of a capabilities approach to animal well-being.

Amid a growing conversation about evolving social norms concerning animals, Nussbaum provides a moral theory for determining what duties humans have to other living things. A particularly useful feature of this theory is its adaptive nature; as information from traditional ecological knowledge or scientific discovery continues to inform understandings of animal ability, the approach can expand rights to creatures not currently considered sentient. Nussbaum has several publications and a forthcoming book that present a moral framework for how people can advocate for animals.

Scientists are also helping people understand animals' minds. Professors Jane Goodall, E. O. Wilson, and Marc Bekoff have popularized a more accurate understanding of animals as complex creatures with cultures and communities. Researchers are finding strong parallels between animal and human behavior in surprising work, as with Mark Rowland's exploration of animal morality, Frans de Waal's discussion of animal capacity, or Barbara King's documentation of animals' grieving.

Animal Property Rights

Philosophers are reimagining human relationships with wildlife through creative new lenses. The 2013 book *Zoopolis: A Political Theory of Animal Rights*, by Sue Donaldson and Will Kymlicka, reconsiders animal rights through the lens of political theory.[63] Donaldson and Kymlicka's now canonical work envisions humans interacting with groups of animals as we interact with groups of people: differentiated by type and subject to universal norms but also with highly individuated rights and responsibilities depending on type.

Donaldson and Kymlicka propose the novel suggestion of granting animals sovereignty over their territories. Sovereignty, they argue, serves to prevent human encroachment on animal habitats—it prevents colonization and invasion and allows for wildlife's self-determination. In this way, *Zoopolis* suggests folding animals into human political institutions at a national level, similar to the idea of incorporating wildlife interests into property regimes, albeit at a different scale of governance and with different implications for protection. For example, property owners generally retain their rights when overarching national governments change. Yet, property owners' interests at the international level differ sharply. In sum, granting wildlife sovereign interests offers a different mix of benefits and costs. The strategies are likely complementary.

Australian philosopher Jonathan Hadley was the first scholar to coin the phrase "animal property rights."[64] In an influential

2015 book, Hadley considered the normative rationale underlying animal property rights—although he is quick to note that his work does not suggest that rights *should* be granted. A specific focus of Hadley's analysis is a basic needs justification for the extension of property rights to animals. Hadley points out "if an individual has an interest that crosses a threshold level of moral importance, then this means they have a right to the goods concerned," and a right to use these goods logically leads to a property right.

Because humans are given property rights for noncritical interests, Hadley argues that animals' interest in natural goods to satisfy their basic needs must at least be sufficient to cross this moral threshold. Under Hadley's rationale, extending property rights to animals would satisfy at least some of the interests of animal rights advocates and environmentalists, since the ultimate result would be preventing (or at least reducing) habitat modification and destruction by humans.

The idea of animal property rights has slowly gained international traction among philosophers. Australian philosopher Steven Cooke is writing on the philosophical dimensions of extending property rights to animals. British philosopher Josh Milburn has constructed a Lockean theory of animal property rights. The emerging question is how animal property rights intersect with the rights of nature.

2

Biodiversity Loss as a
Property Law Problem

Biodiversity loss is a property-based problem. Human land uses are the leading source of habitat loss; habitat loss is the leading cause of species extinction. This dynamic seems simple, but it is absolutely fundamental to understanding the problem of biodiversity loss. The property basis for extinction is hard to see. But clearing a forest to make a field has the same effect on wildlife that a slaughterhouse has for livestock. Making this link explicit is crucial to evaluating existing solutions to stem biodiversity loss, like the Endangered Species Act, and crafting additional solutions.

Land Development → Habitat Loss → Extinction

To highlight the link between land development and extinction, begin with a single example. Imagine that in 1900 your great-grandparents purchased a forty-acre lot in rural Arizona thirty miles away from Phoenix. At that time, the lot was a small piece of open desert, fenceless and largely uninhabited by people. Your relatives raised their three children in a small home on the lot—five people on forty acres. The children moved away; your great-grandparents fenced the lot as neighbors arrived, but theirs remained the only home on the land. When you visited, you enjoyed the unique wildlife on their land: javelinas, roadrunners, bobcats, scorpions. When your great-grandparents died in the late 1970s, their children left the land and house untouched.

Meanwhile, Phoenix grew. In 2010, you were surprised to learn that you had inherited the forty-acre subdivision from your sole remaining aunt. You had not visited the property in years; it had been uninhabited for decades. When you drove to the lot, you were shocked to find that the town of Phoenix had grown into one of the largest cities in the United States. The rural lot of your childhood was surrounded by subdivisions. The animals of your childhood had grown to rely on your family lot increasingly as the habitat around them disappeared.

Imagine that you contacted a realtor and were surprised to find that the lot had become quite valuable, enough to pay for your children's college education. You sell it to a land developer, who builds a subdivision with 160 homes. Soon, over 600 people are living where a family of five once resided, along with hundreds of dogs and cats. The wildlife has gradually gone—pushed out.

In this scenario, you did not want to harm wildlife. Your individual economic interests led you to sell the land, to benefit your family. You likely did not even think about the effects development would have on wildlife. But this dynamic, repeated millions of times, forces wildlife off private land to public lands, where less development occurs. It is not just the creation of subdivisions: draining wetlands, converting forests to fields, and creating roads similarly make land more useful to people and less suitable for wildlife. The cumulative effects over time have brought us to the current moment of crisis, the tipping point of massive extinction that scientists now warn against.

Congress understood the link between land development, habitat loss, and extinction in the 1970s when it enacted the Endangered Species Act. The act requires government agencies to identify habitat particularly important to imperiled species on public and private land. Congress envisioned that the agency and private landowners would work together to mitigate the effects of development on animals. In this way, Congress created a land-based solution to address habitat loss. But the solution imposed a perceived burden on private landowners to maintain species without compensation. Landowners and conservative commentators have fought this dynamic fiercely, so fiercely that agencies massively underenforce the provisions of the act providing for the protection of habitat on private land.

Although commentators focus largely on the Endangered Species Act, Congress unwittingly created a second habitat-protection measure in the 1970s. At the time, neither Congress nor commentators noticed the significance of what they were doing for addressing the dynamic between land development, habitat loss, and extinction. This chapter makes the novel argument that an under-considered Congressional action at the same time may have had tremendous effect on wildlife preservation. And it might provide a model for replicating a land-based strategy for habitat preservation and, thus, biodiversity conservation, through purchasing land for animals.

Ultimately, this chapter suggests that biodiversity loss is a property-based problem. It suggests that adding more property-based solutions (instead of statutory measures, like the Endangered Species Act) might serve to more directly stem species loss.

LEGISLATION IS NOT ENOUGH

In the 1970s, a bipartisan Congress and the Supreme Court aligned to make wildlife preservation a national priority, regardless of the economic harms incurred in doing so. The Endangered Species Act, now a forty-year-old statute, provides the primary vehicle for species conservation in the United States.[1] The act has largely succeeded in keeping species from extinction, but it has also largely failed to address habitat loss, which is the primary threat to animals.

Lessons learned from administering the act are integrated into the property rights regime, which lessens problems such as landowner opposition, state versus federal control, the mismatch between conserving individual species and whole ecosystems, and the distinction between endangered, threatened, and nonprotected species. Admittedly, there is potential for perverse outcomes, such as the intentional extinction of a species to retain human land ownership.

The animal property rights approach highlights the value of vesting animals with property. To avoid widespread extinction over time, either a high degree of land must remain public and managed for wildlife uses, or private property rights, including the right to develop and exclude, must be reduced to provide habitat. Given the political infeasibility of the latter option, the former seems preferable. (It is also more administrable because our government has robust systems of property rights and public lands.) However, the very proponents of strong property rights are presently arguing for dismantling the system of public lands. Such proposals underestimate the degree of public support for wildlife; there is simply a level of diminishment to wildlife that the public will not tolerate. Private conservation efforts alone cannot fill this void.

Many endangered species rely on habitat located on private land.[2] To protect species, federal agencies must conserve their habitat. Agencies do so by exerting control over state and private landowners through critical habitat designations under the Endangered Species Act. Landowners fear that such designation will reduce property values and restrict future development on their property. As a result, landowner opposition has formed the primary barrier to species conservation, creating well-documented public choice effects through which agency officials avoid designating valuable private land as critical habitat.[3] Congressional control of agency budgets creates further incentives for the agency to avoid listing species or designating habitat in the regions represented by key Congressmen. Property owners even destroy habitat or kill soon-to-be-listed wildlife to avoid federal control over their land.

Legal commentators have long understood that habitat loss is a leading cause of biodiversity loss. Population growth, leading to urban sprawl and coupled with industrial land uses, makes much of American land unavailable for animal life. At the time that the Senate was discussing the bill, senators noted: "One of the major causes of the decline in wildlife populations is the destruction of their habitat," and "[f]or the most part, the principal threat to animals stems from the destruction of their habitat."[4] The legislative history of the Endangered Species Act suggests that the sweeping wildlife conservation statute was animated by concerns about habitat-loss caused extinction.

The Endangered Species Act had strong statutory language. The Supreme Court read the statute in an expansive way. However, the reputation of the act as the "pit bull of environmental law" overstates its efficacy over time. In practice, the political economy of landowner opposition has led to Congress diminishing the Fish and Wildlife Service's budget and to political pressures lessening action. The continuous downward funding has hamstrung the Fish and Wildlife Service, rendering it incapable of satisfying statutory mandates without contributions from state, local, tribal, and private partners. As a result, humans are slowly, unintentionally expropriating land from wildlife as an inevitable byproduct of resource competition. The property institutions we have created will systematically, little-by-little remove land from wildlife uses until people make a conscious, concerted effort to do the work to stop them.

The current political climate, coupled with the lived history of the Endangered Species Act, suggests that a statutory approach to animal habitat preservation will not work alone. Instead, a property rights solution can solve this property-based problem. Indeed, at least some of the credit commentators give the Endangered Species Act for species preservation is, in fact, attributable to an unintentional but simultaneous move that Congress made—asserting federal control, with a wildlife habitat focus, over millions of acres of unclaimed homestead lands.

ANTHROPOCENTRIC PROPERTY ALLOCATIONS

Enacting a system of property rights is frequently framed positively, as "creating" rights. The very process of creating property rights for some entails taking away preexisting uses for others. Initial entitlements include creating categories of individuals eligible to own property. The infrequently discussed flip side of this exercise is implicit: it is the process of divesting all who use the resources, which includes both current and future users. Property claimants will seek to establish a protocol for who may own that excludes categories of current users of the land and resources in question (with whom they would otherwise have to bargain for transfer payments).

In our system of property, there exists a latent right for landowners to extinguish customary land uses in any future period, unilaterally and without process. For example, a landowner might allow a neighbor to cross her property to reach a road. Any time the landowner decides to withdraw this permission for a non-owner to use her land, she may do so. If the neighbor refuses to go, the landowner can call the police to remove a trespasser. The police, on behalf of the government, will remove the trespasser, thus protecting the right of the landowner. Among people, the neighbor is entitled to go to court to argue before a judge that her customary usage of the land—long, regular, ongoing—created a prescriptive easement that allowed irrevocable future use. If the judge finds that the neighbor has created a prescriptive easement, the landowner can no longer remove it. The neighbor has the right to continue crossing the private property in perpetuity.

BIODIVERSITY LOSSES—AND MORE

For any individual landowner, excluding wildlife is only problematic for specific displaced wildlife. However, because millions of landowners may push animals off their land over time, habitat shortages become an exponential problem that not only displaces directly affected animals but interrupts entire ecosystems.

The anthropocentric system of fixed entitlements embedded pervasive environmental conflicts into our system of property. Private entitlements divested animals of customary land uses. Much of what property scholars have shuffled into natural resources, such as resource conflicts, the problems associated with monetizing negative externalities associated with land use, and pervasive habitat loss, is explained by the above account, played out hundreds of times across thousands of species.

Our system of property demotes wildlife on land to a resource to be managed, rather than a competing claim holder or customary user. Humans are only one of many animals that rely on natural resources to live, but economic models of resource use systematically exclude wildlife's equal dependence on the same resources.

Anyone who uses a pest control service or mouse trap understands that humans and other animals compete for space. Bugs and rodents are a nuisance, so we push them out of our homes. Fishermen, ranchers, and loggers feel the same about the creatures that compete for space in the ecosystems they harvest. Human-wildlife resource conflict is surprisingly direct when viewed through this lens. Once one begins looking for such patterns of biodiversity loss attributable to human-wildlife resource competition, they seemingly appear everywhere. These examples serve as a reminder that we are simply animals, competing with other animals in the same ecosystem for finite resources.

In recent work, Challie Facemire and I describe this human-wildlife resource competition using the simplified tool of resource triads.[5] This model reenvisions wildlife "management" as interspecies resource competition, with people competing with other species for food, shelter, water, or land. We provide examples of fishermen and sea otters competing for fish, loggers and spotted owls competing for old-growth redwood, cattle ranchers and wild horses competing for forage, and hunters competing with wolves for caribou. In each of these examples, the human resource users kill competing wildlife species to increase human resource consumption.

In the initial periods after land allocation in the West, sparse populations masked the problems resulting from excluding wildlife users. Over time, however, the problems of excluding customary wildlife became clear. Extinction became a large and growing problem. Habitat loss caused by land development is the primary culprit. Congress intervened to offset the problematic distribution in two ways, first through reverting unclaimed lands to public uses that preserved customary animal uses. Second, Congress created sweeping environmental legislation that essentially functioned to revest animal interests in property.

Initial entitlements led to destructive effects on animals and ecosystems. The modern legacies of this problematic system are the back-end attempts to conserve species after destroying a significant portion of their habitat. The result is a clunky system of virtually no protections for most species and over-the-top federal protection for endangered species. The fallacy of species-focused conservation measures is the idea of saving a particular creature, instead of protecting the interconnected ecosystem in which many species coexist. Efforts to save one without preserving the other are nonsensical. Some species in the United States that have been "saved" from extinction live in captivity in zoos; there is nowhere in the wild for them to return.

The Overlooked Importance of Property-Rights Based Solutions

Several scholars and commentators have credited the Endangered Species Act with avoiding species extinction. Commentators have paid relatively little attention to the significance of the nearly simultaneous actions of committing hundreds of millions of acres of land to federal control, with a wildlife focus.

An alternative hypothesis to why species extinction has not occurred at a faster pace may rest in public lands: Did securing ownership rights to land managed (in part) for animal uses also contribute to stemming biodiversity loss? If so, this observation would support the need for ongoing property-based solutions to complement the Endangered Species Act in protecting biodiversity—a vital proposition amid efforts to divest public lands.

Around the same time that Congress enacted the much-lauded Endangered Species Act, it also unwittingly provided a property-based solution to the problem of habitat loss. In 1976, Congress enacted legislation converting millions of acres of unclaimed Western lands to federal ownership. Although this leftover land did not offer the beautiful landscapes found in national parks, the sagebrush-filled deserts provided valuable wildlife habitat. In 1980, Congress enacted further legislation protecting over 157 million acres of Alaskan land with various legal designations—many of which included protections for wildlife. Today, the federal government owns approximately one-third of the land in the United States—roughly 640 million acres. Many of these lands are managed—at least in part—to preserve wildlife habitat.

Wildlife is increasingly constrained to public lands as development encloses private land. When development drove animals from private land, they moved to the less-developed public land. Over time, hundreds of millions of acres of public lands have become functional animal sanctuaries as landowners developed private property. Without this public land, wildlife loss would likely be orders of magnitude worse. Only since the environmental laws of the 1970s have tools like candidate conservation agreements, wetland banks, and conservation easements emerged to protect wildlife on public land. Because people have not afforded animals property rights, their habitat has largely been maintained accidentally, through the preservation of public lands. Agency action to set aside habitat designations on private lands is mired in controversy. In the backdrop, public lands have provided a less dispute-ridden home for wildlife.

Although public land has provided a vital safety zone for nature, it is now under attack at both the state and federal level. In January 2017, Utah Congressman Jason Chaffetz introduced a bill into Congress that called for the sale of public lands to the state. Due to state finances, many of these lands would likely be auctioned off, purchased by private bidders. The recent challenges show the vulnerability of wildlife to shifting laws and public sentiment, reminding us that when only humans can own property, humans can extinguish wildlife rights to that land at any time. Animals are forever in a state of vulnerability, subject to human whims.

From these observations flow two crucial points: the importance of public lands for wildlife preservation, and the potential for benefiting from public lands to expand habitat-based solutions to biodiversity loss. Public lands teach us that setting aside habitat for wildlife is vital, yet public lands are at risk. What other land-based solutions for wildlife preservation might exist?

Part II

Revealing the Existing Body of Animal Property Rights

3

The Biological Origins
of Property

Generations of lawyers, judges, and legislators have assumed the capacity to own property is distinctly human.[1] This chapter challenges received wisdom by linking ethology, the scientific study of animal behavior, to canonical property law doctrines.[2] Animals exhibit behavior that, when undertaken by humans, forms the basis for owning, maintaining, and transferring ownership of property.

"Territoriality" among animals and "property rights" among humans both describe individuals establishing, maintaining, and defending geographical space. Property rights give an owner control over land and objects vis-à-vis other members of society.[3] Law governs what people may do with their belongings and mediates the relationships between multiple property owners.[4] Core elements of property law include acquisition, ownership, exclusion, dispute resolution, transfers, alienation, and third-party rights enforcement.[5] Collectively, these behaviors form a system of property and vest groups or individuals with property rights.

Admittedly, I am about to cherry-pick a handful of examples from the hundreds I reviewed; this is not an exhaustive exploration. It is designed to introduce nonscientists to the surprising

degree of parallels between animal and nonanimal property. I do
so to make the argument later that resource-driven models of animal territoriality may inform theoretical conceptions of human
property rights.

Set aside the televised notions of fight-to-the-death battles
for land. Animals' property behavior is far more nuanced. Indeed, property behavior is not the exclusive domain of "evolved"
or human-like creatures. Species ranging from nuthatches and
ants to lions and wolves acquire, own, exclude, defend, and transfer land and resources. The existence of property rules appears
widespread, perhaps universal. The content of the rules varies
between and among species, human and nonhuman alike. Humans do not lock horns to resolve issues of trespass; deer do not
hire lawyers. Regardless, comparing ethnography to property literature demonstrates a surprising overlap between the previously
disparate fields.

Observing parallels between human and animal behavior concerning the individual occupation of a specific space leads to
two questions. First, do animals consider themselves as owning
property? Second, should people consider animals as potential
property owners? I leave the first inquiry to the talented group
of scientists and philosophers engaged in exploring animal property rights. This chapter grapples with the second question, addressed through the lens of property law.

Ownership of Land and Things

Land ownership among humans generally operates through a parcel system, in which landowners have the right to use their land
and to exclude others from it.[6] Biologists describe animals as maintaining territories, which are roughly analogous to parcels.[7]

The ability to exclude is core to conceptions of ownership.[8] One
definition of territorial behavior is "aggressive behavior that occurs
repeatedly as a direct response to the location of other individuals,
with associated submissive behavior on the part of those individuals or groups to which the aggression is directed."[9] For example,

sunbirds aggressively chase carpenter bees away from nectar[10] and barred owls exclude spotted owls from their territories.[11]

Exclusion is not absolute. Animals may share their territory with offspring, a mate, family, or conspecies (members of the same species).[12] Human and nonhuman species manage property individually, communally, or in a mix of communal and private holdings.[13] Wolf packs and lion prides maintain territories collectively.[14] Within collectively held territories, species can maintain a nested, hierarchical system of ownership, as with a wolf maintaining an individually held home range as a subpart of broader pack-owned territory.[15] Similarly, conspecies occupying the same space may hold property differently, such as with spiders and nuthatches, individual members of which can be floaters or territory holders.[16] Symbiotic species and those within the same food chain can, and must, share the same habitat over time.[17]

Humans participate in shared property regimes with wildlife. For example, some California rice farmers flood empty fields to create habitat corridors for birds during peak migration season to facilitate species conservation.[18] Conservation groups created a "biofence" replicating natural scent barriers to keep African wild dogs from entering human communities.[19] The Boran people of Kenya can determine the location of bees' nests by relying on honeyguide birds' calls and flight patterns.[20] Each of these examples illustrates humans sharing geographic space with animals and using animal communication to further human goals.

Ownership can be temporal with seasonal territories. Several transient species practice site fidelity, in which an animal returns to the same territory year after year.[21] Among humans, seats in the same stadium are granted to both football fans and concertgoers.[22] Both fans and concertgoers would claim to "own" their seats on the night of an event, but neither has a permanent claim. Physical possession matters, too; for example, chimpanzees observe possessory rules for chattel.[23]

Observing parallels between property law and territory studies opens the door to comparative studies of the theoretical underpinnings of property in both realms. Economists and ethologists alike describe property ownership regimes as emerging when the gains of owning private property exceed the costs of ownership.[24] Biologists observe that animals invest more effort in protecting valuable territory but consider the precept of economic defendability, noting that as territory size increases, so too does the cost of defending boundaries.[25]

Acquisition

Acquisition describes how a property owner comes to own a particular piece of property vis-à-vis the rest of the world.[26] Property theorists have historically described the process of acquiring property as beginning in a "state of nature," with no ownership or government.[27] From the baseline natural state, theorists suggest, individuals claim property through discovery, occupancy, labor, or social need for privatization.[28]

Merely entering a landscape is insufficient to establish an ownership claim among either humans or animals.[29] However, possession of chattel—property that is not land—does form an ownership interest among both humans and animals.[30] Social norms and criminalization of theft largely prevent one human from taking another's wallet or computer without permission. Similarly, among primates, such as chimpanzees and monkeys, researchers find "remarkable respect for the rights of the possessor of an object."[31]

Between humans, a transient object, such as a baseball flying through a stadium, must be fully under a person's control before she can assert ownership.[32] Macaques follow similar sophisticated rules of capture; they respect possession when the owner can carry the object in question but not if the object cannot be carried because it was tied to the floor or had a trailing string behind it.[33] Although the context of rules of possession may differ, the existence of property rules with respect to chattel among human and nonhuman species is notable.

Jurist William Blackstone described the transfer from unclaimed land to property as a two-step process: prolonged occupancy and investment of labor.[34] The utilitarian theory of property acquisition suggests property rights encourage labor and investment; John Locke stated, "It is the taking of any part of what is common, and removing it out of the state nature leaves it in, which begins the property."[35]

The prototypical human expression of occupancy is a house or other quasi-permanent dwelling place. Legislation enabling homesteading—the process of converting land from open access to individual ownership—required would-be owners to build a home.[36] This focus on the home is so great that constitutional provisions require the government to compensate limitations on a landowner's ability to build.[37] Constructing permanent shelters is not, however, the exclusive domain of humans. Prairie dogs create extensive underground burrows with tunnels and chambers that serve distinct purposes for family groups (i.e., a breeding pair and children) with defined sections for raising young, sleeping, and defecating.[38]

In addition to creating structures on a property, one could imagine animals hunting as a utilitarian investment in land. Animals hunting prey within their territory satisfy a necessary function of balancing an ecosystem. For example, when apex species like wolves are eliminated from the landscape, deer populations increase unsustainably.[39] By merely carrying out the hunting necessary to survive, species contribute their labor to the natural landscape. Just as farmers "work the land," animals invest labor through regular hunting of their territory.

Exclusion

Some modern theorists describe the right to exclude as the defining feature of property ownership. Animals and non-human animals remain "ever ready to protect that property against aggressors, even to the extent at times of sacrificing [their] own [lives] if necessary."[40] To avoid such extremes, animals practice a variety of territorial behaviors to communicate boundaries and enable noninjurious dispute resolution, both of which are described below.

Boundaries communicate ownership; animals and humans create them in a variety of ways. Ten thousand years ago, preliterate agricultural societies in the Fertile Crescent used pegs to mark property borders.[41] In the United States today, humans predominantly use fences to mark boundaries. More creative local variations also exist: property scholars frequently discuss an example of Chicagoans establishing a claim to a snowy shoveled-out parking space by placing a chair in the cleared space.[42] Such visual signals, as opposed to smells or sounds, provide markers that can be observed from a long distance by human eyes.[43]

Animals also create visual markings, which, although varied in form, can be strikingly similar to human fences. Jaguars create mounds, or large piles of leaves and debris four to five feet in diameter; these appear to be exclusively to communicate territorial boundaries.[44] Visual markers may also be temporary.[45] Robert Ellickson provided as a human example the idea of someone doing a jig in a town square to signal occupancy.[46] This fanciful example finds real parallels among lizards, which use various tail positionings and movements to signal the type and strength of ownership claim on property.[47]

Species also employ olfactory boundary markers, as with scent markings around the edge of a territory.[48] Biologists suggest scent markings essentially construct a "chemical 'keep out sign' or fence."[49] For example, the female Eastern carpenter bee secretes a substance near nest site entrances to establish territory.[50] Wolves and mountain lions create 6- to 12-inch scrapes on the ground and leave urine, feces, or anal gland secretions to create combined visual-olfactory boundary signs that mark the edges of territories and rendezvous sites.[51]

Much like an elaborate, decorative fence with a security gate might indicate a wealthy owner by signaling the ability to incur high costs, scent markings also communicate information about the territory owner.[52] Scent contains a temporal aspect: fresh marks show the age of the claim. It also reflects a well-established boundary—"that the marker is both successful in competition with other animals and has successfully held the territory long enough to mark it." Would-be intruders can discern the social status, health, and nutrition of the marker from its scent. In this way, scent markers convey information to would-be trespassers about the potential cost of intrusion.

Vocalizations are another kind of boundary marker.[53] For example, wolves convey their size and aggressiveness through quality of voice.[54] This is an implicit threat, making it clear the pack could defend its territory if necessary. One can liken animal vocalizations to a human property owner telling a trespassing neighbor to "get off my lawn!"

In sum, animals and humans alike use a variety of visual, olfactory, and auditory markers, sometimes in combination, to mark the boundaries of land they control. Markings communicate exclusivity to conspecies and other species; they can also be observed by predators and parasites.[55]

DISPUTE RESOLUTION

Law has long been understood as an alternative to physical violence in resolving property disputes.[56] Nevertheless, nonviolent dispute resolution strategies are not the exclusive domain of humans. Several species engage in ritualized aggression, or nonharmful physical signaling, designed to ward off trespassers.[57]

One common form of ritualized aggression occurs in response to trespass, or when one potential claimant enters territory claimed by another.[58] In one example, humans and animals challenge property claims by intentionally destroying boundary markers set by others. In the American West, ranchers historically challenged property claims by "cutting fence"—cutting the strands of barbed wire strung between posts.[59] In 1883, Texas cattle ranchers engaged in a "fence cutting war" over a dispute about whether ranchland should be enclosed or open range. Bands of men cut barbed wire fences at night and burned the pasture land of offending ranchers. The fence cutting war generated over $50 million in economic damages. Animals similarly challenge claims to territory through overmarking the scent of competing territory owners or intruders.[60]

Many species adjust their enforcement of property boundaries depending on the identity of the trespasser. Humans may let their neighbors' children encroach on their lawn to fetch an errant ball without comment but will be more aggressive if a group of unknown youngsters gathered on their property. This example extends to a general distinction between familiar and unfamiliar property intruders. Robert Ellickson famously introduced the notion that close-knit communities of neighboring landowners operate in an extralegal system governed by norms, not law, which function to preserve relationships among community members as closer than those of strangers.[61] Ethologists describe a similar "dear neighbor effect" in which two neighboring territorial animals become less aggressive toward one another after territorial borders are well established.[62] For example, new blackbirds settling into a colony interact more aggressively with their neighbors than do familiar blackbirds.[63]

Neighbors do not always get along. Property law cases provide examples of spite fences,[64] built to annoy a neighbor, or street gangs with rivalrous territories.[65] Similarly, among some animal species, territorialism increases among familiar neighbors: numerous bird species respond less aggressively to recordings of strangers than neighbors.[66] The Eurasian badger responds more severely to own-group conspecies compared to foreign-group conspecies.[67]

Territorial altercations rarely result in death.[68] Instead, routine property incursions are more often resolved through nonviolent means—generally physical posturing that rests at the intersection of signaling ownership and repelling an outsider. Before fighting, for example, fish swim around an intruder in warning to create currents pushed toward the adversary.[69] Competing spiders use vibration cues transmitted through the web to compare body size, an important predictor of who would win a fight.[70]

Animals widely rely on the use of low-cost aggression to resolve territorial disputes. Some butterflies, damselflies, spiders, and lizards rely on chases and displays.[71] For example, some lizards use back-and-forth tail signaling to resolve which of two competitors will succeed in claiming territory.[72] Ants undertake ritualized posturing that resembles up-and-down fighting motions instead of actual physical altercation.[73] Some theorize that territorial defense originated in a common ancestor shared by birds and lizards, given the ubiquity of vocalizations and head bobbing in territorial defense behaviors across these species.[74]

When fights occur among nonhuman animals, residents tend to have a competitive advantage over intruders—an observation that is true among certain birds, fish, insects, and crustaceans.[75] Territories, like land parcels, are in a generally stable, but vulnerable, equilibrium. Economists have posited that in a state of nature without legal institutions, claims of property are "individually provided [through] coercive force" and redistribution occurs through aggression.[76] Animal behavior largely undermines this assumption, however, suggesting that social systems of norms, cooperation, and nonviolent dispute resolution exist across a variety of animal species.[77]

Property Transfers

Many potential property conflicts are resolved before they arise because of ingrained rules governing the transfer of property. Transfer rules avoid resetting the status of ownership to "unowned" when a landowner dies and instead give the property to another individual.[78] Much to the dismay of law students studying for the bar exam, humans have developed complicated rules governing how property transfers when its owner dies. Animals, too, have default rules governing intergenerational property transfer that vary by species. Jeffrey Stake has suggested some probate laws are biological in origin by analogizing rules to animal ownership.[79]

To provide a few new examples, jaguars follow matriarchal property transfers, with female offspring sharing the home range of the mother jaguar, whereas young males are forced out of the territory.[80] This intergenerational property distribution system may allow jaguar populations to naturally sustain an appropriate population distribution across landscapes relative to the available natural resources.[81] Similarly, the Seychelles warbler, a bird, remains in the same territory for life, which is subsequently inherited by descendants according to the age, status, and affiliation of male offspring. Inheritance rules may maintain utilitarian investments in a landscape, such as when prairie dogs transfer warrens to their young, or internalized wealth, such as when members of a herd benefit in old age from structures they created or maintained during the prime years of their life.[82]

Fish also follow ingrained patterns of territory use. Red band trout, for example, return for generations to reproduce where they were spawned.[83] Similarly, "Chinook salmon roam over thousands of miles in the ocean feeding and growing for two to five years before they mature sexually and return to their home river to spawn."[84] This is a system of an internalized natural order with benefits traditionally attributed to governance or cultural norms when observed in humans.

Distinctions: Formalized Third-Party Enforcement and Alienation

Human and nonhuman animal systems of property do not appear to diverge much with respect to fixed entitlement or communal enforcement of property rights. The key areas of divergence are formalized third-party enforcement and alienation.

Once fixed, entitlements can be notably difficult to dislodge. Ant colonies with established territorial claims, for example, are almost always able to fend off claims from competing colonies.[85] When colonies fight over unclaimed land, however, the success rate is about even. Stable entitlements are likely evolutionarily efficient, with the stability of property rights enabling both groups to focus on tasks other than constantly defending territory.

Ethological literature does not yield an example of animals relying on third-party adjudicators to decide competing claims. Instead, claims are frequently determined in a Darwinian manner: one species physically prevails over another to assert ownership, albeit often in a ritualized manner. Among humans, Darwinian ownership contests are only partially criminalized; more than half of US states have "stand-your-ground" laws, which allow a property owner to kill an intruder on her property solely on the basis of trespass.[86]

Alienation, or the ability to sell property, forms the strongest distinction between human and nonhuman animal systems of property. Among humans, the right to transfer property is a core tenet of economic and legal understanding of property.[87] Review of the scientific literature does not reveal a market system for real property among any animal species for any good, particularly property. Thus, the markedly different land use patterns among humans and animals likely flows from this distinction. Humans, unlike animals, claim property far in excess of individual needs because it can be traded for other valuable goods on the market.

4

Uncovering Animal Rights in Existing Property Law

A pluralistic view of history and religion shows a legacy of animal property rights across time and place. Native American conceptions of property rights with respect to animals may have included animals as coequal rights-holders with people. Steve Pavlik notes that many North American indigenous groups' "creation stories and laws do not elevate humans above Animal or Plant People." (There are significant variations among groups concerning the content of the creation stories, systems of property rights, and structures of government and governance.) One articulation of indigenous customary understandings of humans' lack of centrality in systems of sharing resources is illustrative:

> What is this you call property? It cannot be the earth, for the land is our mother, nourishing all her children, beasts, birds, fish and all men. The woods, the streams, everything on it belongs to everybody and is for the use of all. How can one man say it belongs only to him?[1]

Moreover, many of the colonial laws imported to the United States also had a place for animal property rights, reflecting the Christian perspective that animals and humans share Earth's resources as coparticipants with equivalent knowledge. In medieval France, Italy, and Switzerland, local officials brought class action lawsuits against insects and rodents who occupied land.[2] Courts held elaborate trials against animals, in which the animals appeared in court and were represented by skilled lawyers.[3]

Later, laws in the United States created protections for animals. Colonial courts adopted the British common-law doctrine of *fera naturae*, which grants wildlife rights of passage over private lands.[4] In 1868, President Ulysses S. Grant set aside the Pribilof Islands in Alaska to provide a protected home for the northern fur seal, restricting human land uses in deference to an animal user.[5] In 1903, President Theodore Roosevelt issued an executive order establishing the Pelican Island Migratory Bird Reservation. Establishing animal reserves did more than create sanctuaries where people could not hunt animals; it created permanent habitat and thus an implicit property interest for animals in the land. By restricting the ability of people to act in certain ways, the laws essentially grant protections to animals that function similarly to how property rules limit human conduct.

Early legislatures and courts also granted animals rights to chattel and natural resources. In 1904, the New York legislature passed a law prohibiting people from disturbing "the dams, houses, homes, or abiding places" of wild beaver.[6] In *Barrett v. State of New York*, a New York court interpreting this law noted that legislatures could protect animals, which could then take property from individual persons, noting: "Deer or moose may browse on his crops; mink or skunks kill his chickens; robins eat his cherries."[7] The court went on to hold that property owners could not recover against the state for the value of trees felled by protected beavers. Similarly, today, the government does not reimburse ranchers for livestock killed by endangered species, and landowners may not cut down a tree in which a bald eagle has nested.[8]

Congress has granted animals property-right-like interests in land, both public and private, for over one hundred years. Below, I review a variety of statutes that grant animals such interests. However, first note that the outer limits of Congress's constitutional authority to extend animals' property rights remain untested. The Supreme Court has never ruled that a congressional grant of rights to animals violated either the Property Clause or Commerce Clause of the Constitution.

Congress has vested wildlife with rights to public land that would comprise legally cognizable property rights if afforded to humans. Although some might suggest that animals merely have possessory rights on public lands, the same is true for any right to use public land, as Congress may eliminate that right either directly or by divesting the land in question.

For example, the National Wildlife Refuge System, which includes over 150 million acres of public land, exclusively focuses on managing the land for fish and wildlife, albeit for the benefit of people:

> The mission of the System is to administer a national network of lands and waters for the conservation, management, and where appropriate, restoration of the fish, wildlife, and plant resources and their habitats within the United States for the benefit of present and future generations of Americans.[9]

More broadly, Congress has used its Property Clause authority to designate over 84 million acres of national parks as wildlife preserves as a result of the Organic Act:

> [To] conserve the scenery, natural and historic objects, and wild life in the System units and to provide for the enjoyment of the scenery, natural and historic objects, and wild life in such manner and by such means as will leave them unimpaired for the enjoyment of future generations.[10]

Preserving wildlife habitat is one of five objectives for the Multiple Use Sustained Yield Act, which covers millions of acres of public timberland and lands managed by the Bureau of Land Management. Similarly, Congress has also granted land to individual species, such as granting a herd of wild horses 31,000 acres in the Pryor Mountains of Montana. Congress has also wielded its Commerce Clause authority to enact several statutes allowing agencies to purchase and manage land on behalf of animals. For example, Section 5 of the Endangered Species Act authorizes the secretaries of the Department of Interior and the Department of Agriculture to acquire "lands, waters, or interests therein" to "establish and implement a program to conserve fish, wildlife, and plants."[11] Congress authorized the secretaries to acquire land through purchase, donation, or "otherwise."

The Endangered Species Act references previous acts in which Congress authorized agencies to buy land to promote the protection of fish and wildlife resources, including the Fish and Wildlife Act of 1956, the Fish and Wildlife Coordination Act of 1934, and the Migratory Bird Conservation Act of 1929.[12] These statutes allow government agencies to purchase land, water, and other property rights for the sole purpose of benefiting fish, wildlife, and plants. Collectively, these statutes demonstrate Congress using its authority under the Commerce Clause to purchase and manage land for animals.

Similarly, Congress has used its Commerce Clause authority to create easements for some animal species on private land. Under the Migratory Bird Treaty Act, a human may not disturb a tree on land she owns if it contains a bald eagle or golden eagle nest, regardless of whether a bird is occupying the nest. When the eagle invests the labor in building a nest in the tree, it creates a de facto property right superior to the de jure right of the human landowner. The Endangered Species Act also permits agencies to designate private lands as critical habitat for endangered species. This designation requires landowners to evaluate the effect of their land uses on the endangered species and sometimes to curb activity in the animals' interest.

Congress also authorized agencies to pursue tort claims for damage to animals and animal habitats under the public trust doctrine. Specifically, natural resource damage provisions contained in six statutes require the government to assert tort claims on behalf of the public for animals whose habitats are damaged by specific environmental harms, such as chemical spills on public lands.[13] These provisions require the tort-feasor to pay damages based on the perceived value of such claims; collected funds may only be used to benefit the injured species directly through programs such as habitat improvement.

The Property Clause of the Constitution grants Congress broad authority to land within the United States:

> Congress shall have Power to dispose of and make all needful Rules and Regulations respecting the Territory or other Property belonging to the United States. . . .[14]

The Supreme Court has repeatedly held that the Property Clause affords Congress the authority to govern wildlife on federal lands. For example, in *Kleppe v. New Mexico*, Justice Thurgood Marshall, writing for a unanimous Court, noted that "the 'complete power' that Congress has over public lands necessarily includes the power to regulate and protect the wildlife living there."[15]

STATE LAWS

States also afford wildlife expansive property-right-like interests. Wildlife has unrestricted access across private property in every state grounded in *fera naturae*. This doctrine affords animals greater rights to cross private land than humans. (The United States criminalizes human trespass on private property, unlike a handful of European nations in which people may freely access, walk, cycle, ride, ski, and camp on private land that they do not own.) States have also granted animals property rights to water use, sometimes above preexisting human uses. For example, California courts held that fish and wildlife protection is a "reasonable and beneficial" use of water under the terms of the state constitution.[16] In 2009, California passed a package of legislative reforms requiring water flow criteria to protect the resources of the San Francisco estuary ecosystem, essentially granting fish and wildlife water rights.

On a different front, legal thinkers changed the Uniform Probate Code in 1990 to provide that domestic animals—pets—can inherit from their human owners. The majority of states have since enacted pet trust statutes, allowing pets to inherit money and property from humans.[17] Less formally, animals have long been the beneficiaries of property through individuals.

COPYRIGHT LAW

In addition to congressional, state, and private recognition of animals functionally owning property, some nongovernmental organizations are using the court system and unexpected statutes to assert this right. An emerging issue in animal property law is whether animals own the rights to property they create under copyright law.

Naruto v. Slater[18] explores who is the rightful owner of a copyright to a selfie taken by Naruto, a macaque, who took several pictures of himself using an unattended camera left on a tripod. The camera owner, photographer David Slater, claims ownership to the copyright of the image. People for the Ethical Treatment of Animals (PETA) claims Naruto is the rightful owner of the copyright. At the lower court, US District Judge William Orrick presided over the so-called "monkey selfie" case and said from the bench, "This is an issue for Congress and the president. . . . If they think animals should have the right of copyright they're free, I think, under the Constitution to do that."[19]

The Ninth Circuit heard the case on appeal and affirmed the district court's judgment in favor of Slater.[20] The court had three main holdings. First, the court held that PETA did not have "next friend" standing to sue on behalf of Naruto, or any animal, but Congress could authorize expansion of the "next friend" doctrine to include animals through legislative action. Second, regardless, the court held Naruto had standing to sue under Article III of the Constitution because Naruto "suffered concrete and particularized economic harms as a result of the infringing conduct by [Slater]." Lastly, although Naruto had Article III standing, Naruto lacked statutory standing because the "Copyright

Act does not expressly authorize animals to file copyright infringement suits." However, the court noted that Congress has the power to give animals statutory standing through legislation: "if an Act of Congress plainly states that animals have statutory standing, then animals have statutory standing."

This analysis mirrors general agreement among courts and scholars that Congress has substantial untapped authority to formalize and expand animals' legal status.[21] It is indicative of a broader common-law approach to creatively expand recognition of animal property rights.

PRIVATE EFFORTS

Large landowners implicitly or explicitly manage their property partially for the benefit of wildlife. Several nonprofit organizations hold land for conservation purposes, including tens of millions of acres under conservation easements, which contain provisions regarding wildlife and wildlife habitat. The American Prairie Reserve is a public-private effort to develop the largest wildlife conservation reserve in the contiguous United States. Although these disparate efforts are important, they lack an overarching legal framework for describing their efforts. Reframing them in the language of animal property rights can provide that framework.

Part III

A Roadmap for Property Ownership to Benefit Biodiversity

5

Using Legal Trusts to Implement a System of Animal Property Rights

Once we accept that animals have property rights, the next step is deciding how people should determine animal interests to manage their property. There are two steps to this process: first, the general consideration of integrating animal interests into the existing legal system and, second, the specific questions of judging animal interests on a case-by-case basis.

The first step includes adding animals to the growing list of nonhuman entities that the American legal system accommodates through trust laws. As a legal matter, this is straightforward; indeed, it has already happened in most states. In this chapter, I address this concern by briefly sketching trusts as a model for facilitating animal-owned lands (but note that other existing structures might serve similar ends, such as B Corporations or biological conservation easements).

Scientists and philosophers express grave concern about the second consideration: discerning what animals want or need. They correctly note that there are many difficult questions embedded in administering animal property rights, such as the treatment of invasive species. Some say that humans cannot know what animals want, and the hubris of attempting to do so is problematic. Although I readily acknowledge these points, I urge scholars to weigh human determinations of animal interests not in a vacuum but instead against the real-world effects of inaction. The alternative to humans administering animal property interests is either the status quo of animals as nonparticipants in the system of property (which is akin to systematically ignoring animal interests) or asking agencies to make parallel judgments on public lands (which raises parallel problems).

I certainly do not claim to have fully worked out the details of how human custodians of animal rights should resolve specific conflicts. Any single scholar is poorly positioned to answer unilaterally such complex questions; determinations would be highly localized. I do, however, offer an analysis of the institutional structures likely to maximize sound decision-making: interdisciplinary teams familiar with the socioecological context.

Stakeholder collaborations provide a template for trustees managing animal interests. Nobel Prize winner Elinor Ostrom and her progeny have documented thousands of case studies of small groups of locals managing local resources, including sustainably managing wildlife populations.[1] As with stakeholder collaborations, a mix of private governance and judicial oversight can be a backstop against abuse. Animal-owned trusts can draw on the increasingly well-documented success of stakeholder collaborations for reaching decisions about managing land and resources in other contexts.

One approach to managing animal-owned property is the well-established system of trust law.* Under this model, human trustees would manage the land at an ecosystem level for the

---

* Animals could own in a variety of ways other than trusts, such as benefit corporations or through representation provided by a guardian ad litem. The fact that some countries do not have trusts should not be seen as a bar on extending my proposal internationally but rather an invitation for scholars to find analogous pathways responsive to the laws within their existing systems of property.

collective benefit of animal beneficiaries, operating under a fiduciary duty. To ensure consistently sound practices, each trustee would operate under the guidance of a private governance committee, which would regularly update standards requiring best practices. Such practices would operate against the backdrop of judicial oversight under trust law. Trustee selection could be determined on a trust-by-trust basis, so long as it accords with the general principles established by the overarching governance committee and common-law trust principles.

Trustees would manage animal-owned lands for the health of the overall ecosystem. As with any policy decision, trustees would weigh the interests of competing constituencies—here, animals—and make difficult decisions about the winners and losers.

Ecosystem–Level Management

Trusts should manage the animal-owned property at an ecosystem level: a generalized, regional level that considers the interconnection of all living things. The alternatives to the ecosystem approach, such as managing at the individual animal or species level, cannot work for most wildlife. Imagine a system in which each animal on a landscape might receive a share in a broader landholding. Problems with such a granular system abound, beginning with a requirement to establish and maintain a census of animals. Such a census would prove absurdly expensive and burdensome due to animals' incapacity to gather, coupled with their near-constant movements and, potentially, seasonal migrations. Small and highly mobile creatures would likely be underrepresented. This formulation is impracticable because it requires a census to vest all wildlife with property rights at an individual level.

Further, individual vests would inevitably lead to conflict between species regarding land management. Various species have competing needs for prey and habitat. Maximizing landholding to benefit one species may harm or extirpate another. If a nonnative invasive fish, for example, received property rights to water in a lake, its human representatives (discussed below) might leverage

those rights in a manner that would eliminate native fish populations. The diverse and competing land management goals for
individual species would lead to burdensome conflict.

Additionally, migratory animals cannot be readily constrained.
If a species owned land in one place but subsequently relocated,
how would the species sell or barter their existing entitlement
for land and resources elsewhere? Animals, lacking cognition of
the ownership interests, would regularly create territories outside
the strict boundaries of their landholding in response to changed
conditions. With climate change, animals' traditional territories
are already shifting quickly.

One can, however, imagine limited situations in which vesting
a particular species with rights makes sense. For example, Congress
might convert existing lands held for wild horses to the wild-horse-
only title. Under such a grant, human representatives would manage the land for wild horse interests. If a competing species entered
the landscape—say, bison grazing on the same grassland—human
land managers would exercise the right to exclude the bison on
behalf of the wild horses. Such vesting may be crucial for saving
imperiled species with limited wild habitat, such as captive breeding populations released into the wild.

Hesitancy arises, however, over Congress's ability to pick "winners" and "losers" among animals. Humans have a poor track record of intervening with wildlife. Moreover, if the condition of a
species changes—say, the wild horses become so abundant that
they spread into other lands—flexibility must be built into the
property rights as well, such as the sale of some portion of the land
and resources to other competing species. Public land, the uses
of which can change at the whims of Congress, provides such
flexibility. Additionally, it seems likely that Congressional action
would tilt toward granting land to charismatic megafauna, which
would exacerbate inequalities among species. Mammals would
likely hold vast tracts of land, whereas less popular species would
hold little. Scientific observation suggests such preferences are
unwise because the popular large species depend on the less-
popular species lower in the food chain. The survival of the for-

mer depends on the existence of the latter, making preferential policies damaging to both. For these reasons, I generally set aside the possibility of individual fish and wildlife owning land directly or through a shared system.

Instead, the sensible allocation would vest animals with property rights at the ecosystem level. Each animal would retain a loose ownership interest in a trust managed for the benefit of all animals on the shared landscape. Enrollment into the trust would be unofficial and loosely defined based on mere possession of territory, or a physical presence in the defined area. Wildlife biologists who are experts in animal surveys could affordably gather data about animal populations at the behest of animal land managers. With proper surveying techniques, seasonally or even more temporally disparate animals would nonetheless remain members. The increased popularity of voluntary human participation in scientific data-gathering—crowdsourced data, such as with Christmas Day bird counts—may make this option both affordable and an opportunity to link humans with other animal users on a landscape.

This example prompts another question: Would human animals retain a right among other creatures within the landscape? Could we use the land for recreational purposes, say hiking or hunting in animal-owned lands? These are complicated questions that would depend on the individual title of lands in questions. For example, public lands cotitled in animal trusts (an option, not an obligation under this proposal) would include both human and animal interests. Private lands maintained by people would not change unless the owners wanted to add wildlife to their titles through biological easements (a form of a conservation easement, affording specific uses to specified animals) or sell to an animal trust. Once people titled private land to animal owners, the trustees could define use rules about who could enter their property. Some trusts might allow humans, and others might not. Similarly, the basis for affording rights might define the rights afforded. If the preexisting property laws of indigenous communities were the basis for rights, the answer might be that humans function as one of many animal owners in the landscape.

Management Risks

I will pause here to note what has thus far been implicit: This proposal stops at property ownership and does not afford the full suite of human rights to animals. Accordingly, animals could still be shot, trapped, and exterminated under an expanded property rights regime. Josh Milburn suggests that human potential to legally kill animals negates the viability of an animal property rights regime, assuming that people would merely kill the animals to take their property.[2] The same could be true, of course, for humans killing other humans to take their property— something we prevent through laws against homicide. I see Milburn's observation as an opportunity to craft sensible laws to resolve the potential problem, not a basis for eliminating the proposal. Dean Lueck's work on the state regulation of hunting shows a centuries-old history of states regulating humans' ability to kill animals. There is no reason such laws could not be crafted to extend protections surrounding property law. Absent such laws, people would no doubt kill other people to take their property. Nevertheless, our legal system has developed laws to prevent this; there is little reason for pessimism about extending such laws to animals.

This reality highlights the need for new laws to prevent property-hungry humans from eliminating broad swaths of the animal kingdom on desirable land. Existing laws about hunting limits would remain, as would the vital protections of the Endangered Species Act. Indeed, the threat of species becoming listed as threatened or endangered would chill extermination, since existing laws would afford a much higher level of protection to the remaining animals.

Still, one must be mindful of the propensity of Congress to change laws. If Congress enacted an animal property rights regime and then repealed the Endangered Species Act, animals would be dependent on state hunting regulations to preserve their populations. If states strategically repealed hunting regulations, property-rich animals might be targeted by humans for widespread elimination to lessen wildlife claims to the animal-owned property. Humans would act as an invasive species, taking over the property.

Importantly, however, human representatives managing the property on behalf of the animals could impose private rules to halt a human invasion, just as they might do with an invasive species on the land. Anglo-Saxon legal tradition allows private landowners to limit and license the use of their property and to determine the appropriate uses of that land independently. Consequently, animal land managers might impose strict limitations on hunting, employ game wardens to enforce the limitations, and use trespass or tort law to recover from offending humans. Property rights would vest in animals a right to self-preservation on their land independent from the whims of congressional or state protection. The concern, of course, rests in the ability of land managers to discern animal desires while avoiding capture by human interests, which I discuss below.

Animal Participation in Human Institutions

A crucial aspect of this project is determining how animals would handle the legal and practical functions of property ownership. Purists might suggest animals should self-manage property, both on the ground and concerning legal interests. Even small creatures like prairie dogs and blackbirds successfully exclude humans from their territories. In a natural environment, apex predators like bears and wolves might be enough to exclude or control human infiltration of land successfully, but such exclusion requires enforcing animal rules and norms against humans on animal-owned land (such as not allowing guns). Then, the problem is interspecies communication.

Animals are incapable of communicating such detailed rules to humans and enforcing them. However, property law and ethology—the scientific study of animal behavior—reveal surprising parallels between human and animal systems of property rights. Some animal behavior reflects what we consider property ownership.

Thus, behavior with respect to property, long described as innately human, may instead be animal in nature. Perhaps most notably, animals can create, follow, and enforce property rules among members of conspecies and even in some interspecies disputes. Natural hierarchy, for example, alerts lower-level animals to the need to avoid higher-level animals, reducing incidents of forceful exclusion through killing, such as with prey observing the boundary markers of predators. Such communication can be bidirectional, but it is rough and based on avoidance.

Humans and other animals have shared property in the wild for the whole of human existence and continue to do so. Modern hikers watch for signs of bears, such as prints, scrapes, or scat, to avoid them; people sing or wear bells in the woods to avoid interactions. Campers and backpackers take care to keep food that might attract bears in impenetrable smell-proof containers to lessen the incentive for bears to enter the campsite. However, new technologies and superior human force lessen our sensitivity to such signals. Bears who venture into suburbs are trapped and released in more wild areas. Humans venturing into nature may take guns or pepper spray to ward off an attack. Although technological innovation has granted our species the upper hand in a confrontation, hikers still sing.

An extreme approach to resolving human-animal conflict on animal-owned lands might require humans to engage in resolution on the terms of the challenged animal. Imagine humans wearing prosthetic antlers when they want to turn a meadow into a campground, challenging the deer who might object to the proposal on its terms. Although this seems outlandish, it highlights a largely unstudied question of how different animal species resolve territorial disputes. Absent biological information that serves as a template, two options emerge: either humans must engage animals on their currently unknown terms, or animals must engage humans on their terms.

The difference, essentially, between animal and human approaches rests on institutions and force: law, markets, and guns. Either humankind must agree to live absent law and markets on animal-owned land by taking no more than they can individually consume and resolving disputes without courts, or they must force animals to resolve conflict on human terms in courtrooms and through market solutions. As a pragmatist seeking fast action to reverse endemic habitat loss, I favor the second approach—folding nature into our existing institutions.

For centuries, humans have insisted on our collective superiority over animals, which a mere extension of property rights is unlikely to change. Humans likely would force animals to participate in our institutions under a property rights regime by defending interests in courts and through lobbying, selling the resources on land at market, and enforcing rules through weaponry. Appointing human trustees to serve animal interests could take a variety of forms, depending on the legal structure of animal interests. There could, for example, be animal corporations, animal real estate investment trusts, or trusts established on behalf of animals.

Animal participation in the human legal system presents a vivid concern: it necessitates the use of human representatives to operate on behalf of animals in government and markets. Legally, humans already can and do represent animal interests under certain conditions. As Laurence Tribe has pointed out, we allow similar representation for the mentally incapable, children, corporations, and even ships.[3] Existing legal institutions can accommodate human representation of independent animal rights, although precedent is mixed on this point. The source of concern, then, arises from a mix of practical, moral, and scientific issues.

Animal Representatives, or Trustees

Practically, granting animals property rights would require articulating who may serve as a legal representative and what duties they owe to animal clients. This is relatively straightforward, given the many analogies in current law, along with existing animal trusts. One would also need to secure enough qualified representatives to satisfy fiduciary duties to animal clients appropriately;

problems with this model abound. Regardless, universities across the country teach land management to generations of foresters, farmers, and rangeland managers. Wildlife and conservation biologists have similar expertise in how to shape a habitat to maximize animal interests.

Should land managers employ these techniques to maximize some element of animal well-being, along some dimension? Who among competing fields should represent animals? With these threshold issues addressed, the real practical issues emerge, namely (1) that people hostile to animal interests would "capture" the trustees of animal-owned lands and (2) that even well-meaning trustees might impute human wants and values onto animals.

The arduous task is determining *how* humans would determine animal interests. Corporate forms are human creations designed to serve shareholders, operating under the long-agreed-to standard of maximizing shareholder value within legal limits. When representing the interests of mentally incapacitated people, trustees operate under shared humanity.

Animals, by contrast, are independent creatures: not human creations, not necessarily designed to serve human interests, and with an existence outside the human capacity to imagine. There is no accepted metric by which to serve their interests best. Articulating such a metric, even on the advice of biologists, necessarily imputes human values into the unknowable mindset of animals. Human imputation of values to animals, known as anthropomorphism, is anathema in the biological community, which maintains that animals are distinct creatures that cannot be understood in relation to humans.[4] Nevertheless, discerning animal interests in land requires precisely such an exercise. There are two responses to this concern: one pragmatic and the other ethical.

Pragmatic Answers

How can humans assess what is in the best interests of animals so that they can manage lands accordingly? This question demands interdisciplinary answers: it is ethical, philosophical, scientific, and legal. Fortunately, philosophers, legal scholars, and ethicists began the conversation at least several decades ago (as discussed in chapter 2). Here I attempt to add a doctrinal element to the discussion by sketching the governance and institutional structures that might create procedurally appropriate bodies to determine these interests.

I argue that all animal trusts should be subject to a single certification regime comprised of a predetermined group of animal experts, such as conservation biologists and indigenous representatives. People creating specific trusts could include a requirement that the trust maintains perpetual certification. The certification regime would be made up of a standing, collaborative group that could create rules for all animal trusts in response to unpredictable and unknown social, economic, and biological changes.

This approach creates several benefits. First, it creates a single, transparent set of guidelines that trustees, the public, and courts can review. Second, it threatens trustee transfer under conditions of improper management. Third, the existence of a standing group avoids issues of statutory ossification and allows flexible rules responsive to changes over time. Still, the problem of how the group would discern animal interests at the ecosystem level persists. To some degree, the relative consensus among evolutionary biologists that animals exist to survive as a species across generations mitigates this concern. Perhaps this could become the standard duty of human trustees, but prioritizing the survival of various species or ecosystems requires thousands of nested decisions (or, at times, nondecisions), each of which must be determined based on human actors' guesses and priorities.

Ultimately, mismanagement of animal lands is a serious concern. Existing corporate, trust, and fiduciary standards would govern the various forms of ownership. A legal standard would eventually emerge for how human custodians would promote the best interests of rights-holders, potentially drawing on analogies from the corporate form or custodians for children or the differently-abled. Inevitably, some trustees would mismanage animal lands over time. For example, people might barter or sell property rights in ways that were not beneficial to animal owners. Animal claims would likely be subject to growing pressure to sell due to human population growth. Agencies as land managers might also give rise to the potential for capture by interest groups, a concern some would argue already plagues how the Fish and Wildlife Service administers the Endangered Species Act.

The coexistence of publicly managed and privately held animal lands provides a mix of benefits and harms. Redundancy is valuable in high-stakes systems to protect against failure within one system. As applied to animal-owned land, public lands could backstop management mistakes on private lands and vice versa. For example, if a future Congress uniformly divested animals from formerly public property—which seemingly would run afoul of takings law, but has happened in the past to some groups—the remaining privately titled land would provide a backstop for animal interests. Moreover, private animal landholding groups would not be subject to congressional budget variations and limitations of public finances, a genuine concern associated with agency management of animal lands. A uniform public-private regime would produce economies of scale that would serve to reduce administrative costs by having one overarching private body oversee all animal-owned lands against the backdrop of judicial protection through trust law. Information costs and coordinated national strategies might also be easier to form through a private regime.

Open Questions

An animal property rights regime would initially increase the burden on courts to accommodate the new idea of animals as property owners. Property scholars would likely be interested in how courts would resolve competing doctrines that would emerge with animals as property owners. To consider one example, landowners have long sold hunting rights for third-party hunters to shoot game on their property. However, a distinct property doctrine prohibits humans from selling their bodies in part or whole; in most jurisdictions, one may not sell cells, organs, sex, or children.

Could animal property owners sell hunting rights for humans to kill some members of their entrusted animal species in exchange for money? Does the calculus change if animals were the beneficiaries of the monies generated? Would it be ethical to allow animal trusts to generate funds by allowing some degree of hunting on trust lands? Under existing societal norms, this would likely be acceptable; shifting mores over time might require updating the approach.

The above set of questions provides one example of several unresolved legal questions that would likely emerge from an animal property rights regime. This observation does not definitively suggest that the cost to the courts would exceed the societal benefits of an animal property rights regime. Instead, it highlights the issue as one of many that demands scholarly attention.

Trustees would not need to manage animal-owned lands in the same way that agencies currently manage public lands. Indeed, diverse land management approaches might be beneficial in studying innovative practices. For example, one approach to animal-owned land would be to allow it to revert to a "state of nature" with minimal human influence. Under such a regime, fires would be allowed to burn without human-directed replanting. People would not cut down trees. Although such a return to nature sounds somewhat idyllic, one must recognize that a no-intervention policy would, at times, produce unpalatable results: some species would go extinct; others would burn to death in fires. Nature has a long time-horizon on land management.

Further, the animal-owned property would be subject to existing statutes; managers would need to follow Endangered Species Act protections and other statutory provisions. Moreover, an inactive management strategy might produce tort liability. Sovereign immunity protects government land managers from tort liability for management decisions that disfavor neighboring landowners. Animal property owners would not benefit from sovereign immunity, and thus may face tort liability for allowing, for example, a heavy fuel load of trees to accumulate on their property.

6

Traditional Legal Pathways to Formalizing Animal Property Rights

In addition to pragmatically retitling lands, wildlife advocates can also serve the broader goal of animal property rights through legal and political action. This chapter briefly outlines three such pathways: (1) a statutory approach through which Congress or state legislatures explicitly acknowledge animal property rights; (2) a litigation approach advocating for animal interests overlaying public and private lands; and (3) a litigation approach focused on enforcing property-based protections for animals in existing federal statutes.

Statutory Approach

Congress or state legislatures could enact a statute or constitutional amendment explicitly establishing animal property rights. Every scholar or court that has examined the issue of animal standing has decided that Congress has the authority to enact such a statute. Several national governments worldwide have enacted constitutional amendments granting rights to nature. This would represent the clearest, most direct path toward animal property rights—sidestepping questions of standing and eliminating judicial confusion about animal-owned lands. Yet, given the nascent nature of animal property rights—an idea that has emerged only within the past decade—advocates might believe that enshrining the right in law too early might diminish future efforts.

Although Congress could definitively establish animal property rights (or rights of nature and standing for animals), that seems unlikely given the current political climate. Indeed, the more relevant question might be whether Congress could act to eliminate animal property rights. Congress could eliminate government-granted rights to wildlife on public and private lands by amending or repealing statutes. Indeed, recent proposals to divest some federally owned lands may ultimately have this effect.

Interestingly, however, Congress cannot eliminate animals' private property without paying just compensation to the animal owners. The Fifth Amendment to the Constitution, which contains the Takings Clause, provides that the government must pay just compensation when taking private property. If Congress enacted a law banning animal ownership of land, it would be required to compensate current animal property owners for the land. In this way, a system of private lands benefiting animals are less subject to Congressional will than a system wholly dependent on public (or government-owned) lands serving as wildlife habitat.

Litigation to Expand Rights

Animal advocates could seek to expand the body of precedent explicitly recognizing expansive property rights for animals in courts. This rights-expansion could range from protecting an individual animal, such as a domestic cat or dog, to a wildlife species or even ecosystems in a collective rights regime. The litigation model would include wildlife agencies and nongovernmental animal-rights or conservation organizations that challenge uses of public lands in which animals are arguably owners.

Litigants could advance a customary rights argument for animal property rights. One can imagine two customary approaches that would vest wildlife with property rights, the first of which reflects the Native American custom of land ownership, and the second of which acknowledges animals as having customs worthy of legal protection.

Custom is a long-standing, although rarely invoked, legal doctrine that allows local custom to supersede the common law if the customary right "existed without dispute for a time that supposedly ran beyond memory, and [was] well-defined and 'reasonable.'"[1] The most technical definition of immemorial uses requires the practice predate the reign of Richard I, which began in 1189. Early American courts hesitated to adopt customary practices, noting there was no local law preceding the common law that British settlers imported with them. That reasoning overlooked the existence of a robust set of Native American laws and customs, which predated colonial settlement and likely satisfied the English common-law test of developing before the twelfth-century reign of Richard I.

Animal property rights existed in the precolonial United States. Some indigenous governments recognized animals' rights to land and resources as equivalent to humans'. Colonial courts did not know animals had property rights; it simply did not occur to them. As a result, colonists did not think to challenge such rights, and courts never extinguished them. Treaties are highly variable, so it is difficult to generalize, but it seems unlikely that they systematically included provisions transferring animals' interests in land. Dormant for centuries, animal property rights recognized by indigenous peoples are nevertheless still valid.

Latent property rights do not die simply because they are not explicitly recognized, exercised, or enforced. Resource use rights can lay dormant for decades but be judicially enforced in the future. In 2002, the Supreme Court of Colorado issued an *en banc* decision in *Lobato v. Taylor*, holding that the descendants of prior resource users had "implied rights" to "grazing, firewood, and timber" on land they did not own.[2] The court found that the existence of these rights in pre-American land grants coupled with customary resource use, necessity, and reliance to form a "prescriptive easement, an easement by estoppel, and an easement from prior use."

Similarly, in 1995, the Supreme Court of Hawaii ruled that municipalities could only issue permits for land development after finding that the permit will not have "a significant adverse affect" on cultural resources, including "historic sites" and "community activities."[3] The court found that the Hawaiian constitution created a property right to "continued access to . . . property for the legitimate and reasonable practice of customary and traditional rights," which would require compensation if taken by the government. The Hawaiian constitution explicitly recognizes property interests in "all rights, customarily and traditional exercised for subsistence, cultural and religious purposes and possessed by ahupu'a tenants who are descendants of native Hawaiians who inhabited the Hawaiian Islands before 1778." In this way, the constitution prioritizes "established Hawaiian usage" as superior to English common law to resolve a conflict of laws.

The parallels between these decisions and animal property rights rest in rules that preexist land entering into the United States. If lawyers concretely establish that indigenous systems granted animals (or all natural and living things) property interests in the land where they were found, there exists a basis for asserting these rights today. Building on these and similar cases, litigants could advance a customary rights argument for animal resource uses.

A customary approach relying on Native American traditions would likely suggest wildlife in America have sweeping property rights, which they still own and have never had taken away, bartered, or sold. (In the alternative, a more radical formulation would suggest wildlife rights are at least equivalent to those of humans but are considerably weaker than those imported through British law primarily because they are subject to an implicit trust obligation for future generations.)

The infamous case *Johnson v. M'Intosh* reminds us that the US Supreme Court has, virtually since its inception, trounced on Native American custom with respect to property rights.[4] Colonialists expropriated much of American land from Native Americans through property law. In *Johnson*, the court privileged acquisition by discovery, a positive legal approach showing that property rights are established through government and the power of law. This ruling contrasts with a natural law approach, which would hold that legal rights arise as a matter of fundamental justice.

A more aggressive form of the customary argument would seek to establish that animal behavior itself forms a basis for a customary rule of animal behavior. This approach is, admittedly, a massive leap from existing legal doctrine. It would represent a fundamental shift in judicial consideration of natural systems as preexisting, and thus perhaps displacing, human-created law. Law has yet to theoretically or practically reckon with the notion of parallel systems of law among other species. I suspect property represents one of several aspects in which animal behavior shows surprising, undiscovered parallels to human systems of governance.

One benefit of a litigation model is that advocates can implement it with relative ease. Several existing nongovernmental organizations, including the Center for Biological Diversity and the Nonhuman Rights Project, are already experts at carrying out incremental, multiyear litigation to advance broader objectives benefiting nonhuman animals. A litigation-based approach offers, however, slow progress. Richard Posner laid out a roadmap for the nonhuman rights approach to animal welfare, noting that it relies on "show[ing] how courts can proceed incrementally, building on existing cases and legal concepts, towards [the] goal of radically enhanced legal protections for animals."[5] Nevertheless, this line of argument, coupled with the advocacy of indigenous groups advancing the rights of nature, may provide a new pathway toward establishing rights.

Litigation to Enforce Existing Statutory Rights

As discussed in chapter 5, Congress has already enacted many statutes creating property-based protections for animals. If this is true, and property is the solution to wildlife conservation, why is habitat still being lost? The answer rests between law-on-the-books and law-as-applied. In other words, even a strong law can have a limited effect if the agency responsible for administering it does not do so. As an alternative to litigating to revive dormant property rights, environmental nongovernmental organizations or states could also litigate to enforce statutorily created rights. Many organizations are already doing this work, but opportunities exist to take it further.

Such is the case with the Endangered Species Act, which the Supreme Court read as being incredibly strong but which has not fulfilled its promise across decades of agency administration. In practice, landowner backlash has constrained agencies from using the property-based provisions of the act, such as the critical habitat protections. To avoid political controversy, and associated funding effects, the Fish and Wildlife Service has routinely avoided designating private lands as critical habitat for endangered species, even though the statute requires this. Simultaneously, Congress has gradually decreased agency funding to the point that the two administering agencies are no longer able to administer the act as required by the statute. Thus, there exists a gap between what the law requires and what agencies do.

Nongovernmental environmental organizations like the Center for Biological Diversity have engaged in decades-long efforts to sue federal agencies for failing to satisfy their statutory mandates. Judges have required agencies to act. Similarly, private organizations and nonfederal governments are bolstering the efforts of underfunded agencies by providing resources to fulfill statutory aims.

In another example, state and federal agencies collect money from groups that harm the environment through oil and chemical spills to restore damaged natural resources, including wildlife. For example, British Petroleum paid government trustees of natural resources over $8 billion to restore nature after the *Deepwater Horizon* oil spill. Importantly, the authorizing laws require all of these monies to be spent directly on restoring nature. Natural resources damages are not fines; they cannot be used to clean up oil. Instead, they must be used to restore nature to its baseline condition before the responsible party damaged the environment.

Government agencies collect the money for nature based on the public trust doctrine—the idea that the government manages public lands and natural resources for the American citizenry as a whole. If someone "breaks" what the American public owns, that party must "fix" it.

Government administration of natural resource damages is problematic because of information asymmetries generated by questionable settlement practices. At present, the American public that the laws were designed to protect cannot evaluate the damage done to nature. Government trustees virtually always settle these lawsuits, but do so without revealing to the public how much damage was actually done. In one rare situation in which an agency inadvertently released the dollar value of the damage to the public, it became clear that the government settled for pennies on the dollar of the actual damage. Although judges review higher-value settlements, this process is insufficiently democratic to protect trust values.

Moreover, there is limited public oversight on whether funds are spent to benefit wildlife. Even before the *Deepwater Horizon* spill, over $600 million in decades-old, unspent funds were sitting in an interest-bearing account. Wildlife advocates could argue in court that government agencies holding these funds are responsible for spending them as Congress directed: on restoring wildlife populations.

The Endangered Species Act and Natural Resource Damages statutes are valuable environmental statutes. They have both accomplished many wins for wildlife. Nevertheless, the administrative agencies are failing to deliver on what they are statutorily required to do—hamstrung by a lack of funding or insulated by a lack of transparency and public oversight. By litigating to close the gaps between statutory protections for wildlife property and boots-on-the-ground action, wildlife advocates could seek to improve the property protections afforded to wildlife.

7

Leveraging Property Rights to Aid Biodiversity

Chapter 5 provided an overview of one possible structure for animal-owned lands. Remember, however, that property is a tremendously creative tool. People have been innovating through property ownership for generations. Animal-owned trusts are only one model. There are many other avenues that wildlife advocates could use to advance biodiversity. Perhaps most importantly, one generally need not ask governmental permission to use existing property tools to benefit wildlife. (Although the advice of a good lawyer is necessary. This book does not constitute legal advice; one should consult an attorney before using any of the tools outlined in this chapter.)

This chapter sketches a blueprint for several innovative, property-based approaches to improving the plight of wildlife. This transforms the work of wildlife conservation from a rarefied government-led exercise to a democratized approach in which people can individually contribute. It warns, however, that private governance systems need to make sure that these efforts are targeted and effective.

These strategies join a long tradition of people using property laws in creative ways to circumvent unfair social rules that

disadvantaged particular groups. Just as single women and formerly enslaved people creatively wielded property to gain social
and legal standing otherwise unavailable, so too can animal advocates empower wildlife in ways that outpace judicial and legislative movement through the use of property. This encouragement
to innovate should be backstopped, however, by pragmatically
using lessons from other property innovations to maximize its
effectiveness.

1. Creating an Animal Trust Certification

The greatest investment a philanthropist could make to support
this project would be the funding of a robust, sustainable system
for certifying animal trusts. This institutional investment would
do much more for animal rights than any single piece of land.
Stability is a crucial feature of property systems that encourages
investment. Without assurance that donations to animal-owned
trusts would be stable, landowners should be cautious in giving
land to animal owners. But by creating a well-run, centralized
organization to create, record, and administer animal trusts, phi-
lanthropists and social entrepreneurs can leverage existing animal interests and attract future donations to create a sustainable,
lasting impact.

Private governance is a crucial aspect of the successful administration of property rights. Yet the governance systems this
book envisions do not yet exist. Organization is crucial to property. Basic functions like recordation of land grants are scattered
in thousands of county recorders' offices nationally. If people follow the rest of the recommendations in this book without a central organization to coordinate efforts, the ultimate effect of this
proposal will be diminished by structural flaws. An animal property regime will remain fragmented without a national body to
create uniformity through recordation.

There are many available lessons from certification regimes,
conservation easements, and international land recordation that
can model the best practices for animal trusts. Expertise exists.

Establishing a central body to impart these lessons now—at the advent of awareness of animal-owned property—will have tremendous long-term impacts. By adapting lessons from other certification regimes, an animal trust certification would promulgate standards to which all reputable animal trusts would adhere. This system of private governance would create an additional, nonjudicial check on animal trustees to provide uniform management. Donors of property interests to animals could require their trustees to perpetually meet the standards of the trust and pay an ongoing fee to the certifying body to ensure enforcement of the terms of the trust.

As the system of animal property matures, the trust would likely be comprised of interdisciplinary teams of experts working to promulgate rules for trustees to administer animal-owned land. The trust might issue opinions on controversial issues thought to affect many trusts, best practices for trustees, and arbitration of administrative issues. Over time, the certifying body would be financially sustainable based on the annual fees paid by member trusts.

The benefit of this certification would be to relieve the burden on the judicial system, shift certain kinds of decisions from judges to scientific experts, and provide practice, ex ante administrative guidance instead of reactive judicial guidance. It would also imbue flexibility into trusts, so that the trust itself could defer matters that might evolve—such as how to monitor trusts—to the rules of the certifying body, which could update and improve over time. Although I imagine that a well-developed trust would handle most matters, the backstop of judicial administration of trust law is an inescapable feature of a trust. If a trustee acted egregiously in collaboration with a certifying body, a court still could—and should—step in to protect the interest of animal beneficiaries.

2. Conservation Easements

Millions of acres of land in the United States currently operate under conservation easements, in which a landowner has permanently surrendered some development rights in exchange for a tax benefit. Many conservation easements contain a biological easement for specified plant and animal species. At present, biological easements remain lumped with other aspects of the easements, which muddies administration when various interests conflict. Wildlife advocates could create a system of trusts for monitoring the biological aspects of conservation easements, separate from other interests contained within the easement.

Lessons learned from land trust certifications could inform best practices for establishing new biological easements and monitoring existing easements. For example, important work by Jessica Owley notes that the proliferation of forms of easements is problematic. A standardized form for biological aspects of conservation easements would improve the administrability of easements. Similarly, collating currently disparate biological easements under a unified recording system might provide synergistic wildlife management by, for example, highlighting the existence of landscape-level habitat or migration corridors spanning multiple properties.

3. Granting Partial Ownership Rights

Many people may donate or sell partial property rights to animals but not fully relinquish their interests. Real property—or physical property, such as land—can be divided in a number of ways not obvious to a layperson. Property law allows one to sever land from various resource rights in various dimensions.

Two-dimensional property rights—or the straightforward division of land parcels—can readily be divided among several owners. Property owners could establish trusts with joint animal and nonanimal owners. In conservation easements, for example, a landowner agrees to refrain from certain activities to preserve conservation values permanently. Under such an arrangement, the landowner holds certain rights, and the conservation easement holder can enforce negative rights. In many conservation easements, biological easements exist to benefit individual specified plants or wildlife. Biological easements could be considered an animal property right, and subject to trust responsibilities as described above, in addition to a separate private governance certification regime.

Property is also divisible in the third dimension, as with vertical forms of property. Due to the doctrine of the split estate, various owners can own different natural resources associated with the same land parcel. For example, Party A might own a land parcel, Party B might own the water rights associated with that parcel, and Party C might own the air rights. A multitude of resource rights—most of which are severable, or divided among varying owners—run with the land. Wildlife could own a resource, or portion of a resource, on land.

Property is also divisible along the fourth dimension of time. The temporal distribution of property already occurs with wildlife. For example, conservation groups pay California farmers to flood their fields to facilitate bird migration seasonally. Similarly, Kansas farmers sell hunting rights to their fields to sportspeople seasonally. These examples demonstrate farmers providing temporal property rights based on wildlife migration; through leasing programs, similar rights could be granted directly to wildlife according to their needs.

4. Animal Advocates

Some judicial reticence about extending rights to animals rests in concerns of administrability. In the Ninth Circuit case of the monkey selfie, Judge Carlos Bea acknowledged a clear line of precedent that animals could bring claims in their own name. He questioned, however, which legal practitioners might bring such claims. The opinion contained a scathing critique of the nongovernmental organization People for the Ethical Treatment of Animals. Judge Bea questioned whether the organization was acting in the animal's interest or in its own.

To assuage judicial skepticism of lawyers litigating on behalf of animals, leading thinkers in animal law might form a coalition to privately assess animals' interests in a case. Vetting animal interests through a well-respected body prior to litigation would relieve judges of some of the work of assessing the fit between the lawyer and her (nonhuman) client(s). This organization could develop transparent, consensus-based criteria about animal representation to establish norms surrounding payment and fee structures. This might offload some of the work that judges are doing to make such assessments from scratch by establishing a national baseline, allowing judicial focus to rest primarily on the merits of the cases before them.

5. Copyright and Intellectual Property

The concept of property also extends beyond land and resources. Intellectual property is essentially the privatization of ideas. If people are entitled to content and ideas that they produce, so too might be animals. This was the basis of the Naruto, or "monkey selfie," case—that an animal owned a picture that it created.

For example, imagine a world in which sports teams or car manufacturers had to pay into animal trusts for using animal mascots or names. Considering depictions of animals for commercial purposes, a violation of copyright without proper permissions through animal trustees would be a tremendous source of revenue generation, the proceeds of which could benefit animal lands and conservation efforts. Although it seems a stretch of current copyright law to make such claims, leaders in sustainability could undertake voluntary, industry-wide efforts to acknowledge animal contributions to their products.

For example, the Council of Fashion Designers of America has taken a bold, public position on sustainability. One can imagine a campaign in which sustainability-conscious designers would contribute to conservation groups a portion of their proceeds for clothing or accessories bearing animal prints, like a leopard-print sweater.

6. The Giving Pledge for Landowners

"The Giving Pledge" is an initiative started by Bill and Melinda Gates and Warren Buffet in which billionaires commit to give away more than half of their wealth to charitable organizations. The pledge was designed to shift social norms around wealth to emphasizing philanthropy over the intergenerational transfer of wealth among family members. Today, over two hundred of the world's wealthiest people worldwide have joined the pledge.

One can imagine America's largest landowners—such as John Malone or Ted Turner—spearheading a similar pledge to devote a majority of their landholdings to benefit wildlife. This could take the form of either explicit titling of land to animals or placing a permanent biological easement on their land to benefit wildlife.

These examples show a handful of the many creative variations on the theme of animal property rights that could emerge over time.

Case Studies of Stakeholder Collaborations Managing Resource Competition between Humans and Wildlife

This chapter presents three real-world examples of humans managing wildlife interests to add a realistic dimension to the discussion above.

First, I describe an ongoing conflict between cattle ranchers and wild horses in the American West. This presents a deeper dive into the very primal nature of resource conflict—that humans are simply creatures looking to create from natural resources energy for ourselves, the same as every other living thing. I also show how laws—property rights, statutory tools—add flexibility into human interactions, creating a society-wide ability to coordinate action.

The second case study explores expropriation through the story of the thick-billed parrot. What happens after human use of land pushes other creatures off the landscape? A bird that had resided in the American Southwest for thousands of years eventually left Arizona but remained in Mexico. A multiyear effort to reintroduce the species failed spectacularly. Decades later, a federal agency decided to bolster Mexican habitat through funding, rather than attempt again to reintroduce the species in Arizona. In this way, I argue, species are continuously moved to lands with lower perceived values—public and foreign—to avoid conflicting with powerful human interests in resource-rich areas.

The final case study provides hope, in the form of a collaboration among many humans to manage caribou. Following the devastating collapse of enormous caribou herds in Alaska, government officials engaged Alaskan Native communities and other key stakeholders to increase communication and cooperation. The resulting collaboration forms a potential template for the kind of animal trust I suggest in this book. It illustrates that people can work collectively to advance a mix of human-animal interests that benefits species survival in conjunction with human uses. I do not claim this case study is an ideal model; it has faults and weaknesses, which I readily acknowledge. Nevertheless, it shows a flicker of hope in localized governance solutions that can interweave human and wildlife needs into a landscape, rather than insisting that only human needs matter.

Themes emerge across the case studies, underscoring the key points in the book. The first is that humans and other animals exist in constant competition for the Earth's most basic resources. The response to this observation cannot be "eliminate human-animal resource competition"—that is simply unrealistic. Animals competing for space and light and air and food is natural and inevitable—part of a balance that is true across species and lifeforms. The only problem is that we have thrown things out of balance, forgetting the greater whole of which we are part, ignoring the intergenerational wisdom and science that remind us that we exist only as part.

The stories I tell through these case studies show the failure of laws, policies, and theories that neatly divorce humans from the real, biological, natural world. I have interviewed dozens of people to understand their perspectives and worldviews—a diverse cross-section which collectively holds many conflicting beliefs. Yet the most surprising theme to emerge is a fundamental human understanding about nature. Bogeyman discussions about people who do not understand that nature matters seem to be just that—a straw man that oversimplifies complicated perspectives. People understand that nature matters. They understand that a fundamental human question is situating ourselves in this biological sphere. The vocabulary, values, and techniques vary. But the human understanding that we are part of nature is universal. My hope is that building on that embedded sense of nature can lead to more bipartisan, sustainable mechanisms for integrating nature into the spheres that have long excluded it.

The final theme that emerges is that most people care deeply about animals. Horse advocates devote years of their lives to a single species. Their efforts prompted Congress to enact a law for horses, the *New York Times* to run a cover story about them. Volunteers spend years lovingly raising wild birds, training captive-born babies on wild behaviors, and crying when they die. Alaskan Native communities center around caribou. For hundreds of years, they have lived in ecological balance. When caribou were at risk, communities were willing to bridge deep social divisions and distrust with government officials to help them.

And herein lies the flame of hope—something far more than a flicker. The will exists to create vibrant, healthy ecosystems where animals and humans coexist. For a long time, we have treated our institutions as if they need not have that soul—making corporations and laws the vehicles through which we could do things that human morality would not allow us to do individually. That veil is lifting. We understand that we are our institutions, our laws, our companies. Their actions are our values—not something existing in parallel. With that understanding, we can either attempt to deprogram the fundamental elements of human belonging in nature and caring for animals. Or we can update our institutions to reflect the values embedded in us, the evolutionary drive that to survive we must coexist.

Case Study 1: Ranchers and Wild Horses in the West[1]

Wild horses (which people also refer to as "mustangs" or "feral horses") have roamed the American West since domestic horses escaped from the Spanish conquistadors in the 1500s. Early bands of escaped horses roamed on indigenous-owned land. Even today, the line between wild and domesticated horses is fluid. People sometimes capture and domesticate wild horses; they also release domesticated horses into undeveloped lands to join wild herds (which is deeply problematic for a variety of reasons). Scholars and stakeholders hotly debate the appropriate classification of wild horses.

Over the course of generations, human populations grew; so too did numbers of livestock, including cattle and sheep. Ranchers rid vast swaths of the western landscape of predatory animals that could kill livestock, such as wolves or mountain lions. Land became more valuable. Homesteaders logged the land to build homes and farms. Their children engaged in larger-scale mining and forestry. Their grandchildren created subdivisions. Each wave of development fueled economic development but also diminished public goods, such as wildlife, plant biodiversity, forests, and clean water.

Wild horses eat the same forage—grasses, forbs, and shrubs—and drink from the same water sources as livestock. As a result, ranchers poisoned, hunted, and captured wild horses.[2] Ranchers also claimed, fenced, and developed many of the lands that were historically wild horse range.[3] Wild horse populations dwindled.

Conservationists eventually formed a social movement to highlight the plight of wild horses. Velma Bronn Johnston, who earned the nickname Wild Horse Annie, was an early activist. Johnston was a ranch owner with a day job as a secretary for an insurance company. She was driving to work one day when she noticed blood dripping from a truck over-crowded with horses. Johnston followed the truck to where it stopped—a slaughterhouse. She was horrified to learn that the horses headed to slaughter were wild horses.

This experience turned Johnston into a lifelong advocate for wild horses. Within a year, her advocacy led the Nevada legislature to enact a bill stopping planes and cars from rounding up horses. This was a limited victory, however, because more than 80 percent of Nevada is federally owned. The Bureau of Land

Management (BLM) and Forest Service managed these lands and were exempt from the state law. Nevertheless, Johnston persisted. She led a letter-writing campaign that prompted Congress to enact a law banning air and land vehicles from hunting or capturing wild horses on federal land.

In 1971, Congress unanimously passed another act—the Wild and Free-Roaming Horses and Burros Act of 1971—which prohibited people from capturing, injuring, or disturbing wild horses. President Nixon signed this into law on December 15, 1971. This act also set aside public lands as exclusively managed for the use of wild horses, creating a possessory right for wild horses across millions of acres of public land.

The act made it criminal for people to kill, harm, or harass wild horses. Ranchers could no longer slaughter horses that walked onto their land—creating a functional easement for horses to pass through private land. This was a controversial point—ranchers were irate that they had to call federal land managers to collect the errant horses rather than killing them. State public land managers challenged the act, claiming that the Property Clause of the Constitution allowed Congress to regulate only "wild" animals, a status for which wild horses did not qualify. In *Kleppe v. New Mexico*, the US Supreme Court unanimously ruled that Congress had expansive constitutional authority to manage wildlife—broadly defined—on public land. This was a tremendous victory for wild horse advocates.

Today, the competition between wild horses and ranchers plays out primarily on public lands, which the government owns. Public land managers tightly control the uses of forage and water by limiting the number of animal users; without proper management, overuse occurs. Land managers employ flexible controls to limit each user group. Wildlife populations are managed by hunting permits. Wild horses are captured and sold at auction. Livestock are managed through grazing permits issued to ranchers. The controls are flexible enough to allow annual adjustments in each category.

Federal grazing permits are markedly less expensive than state or public permits.[4] Some environmentalists and liberal commentators call cattle grazing "rancher welfare" noting that a very small number of ranchers are receiving an outsized public subsidy.[5]

The difference is even greater with respect to higher-priced permits on private land. A nearly ten-fold difference in price between federal and state grazing permit prices essentially operates as a federal subsidy to ranchers. Ranchers profit from underpriced permits. Indeed, permits are frequently included in the sale of private ranches, even though they ostensibly cannot be issued in future years.

Wild horses and ranchers directly compete for forage and water on public land. Each additional wild horse per acre produces a one-unit deduction in the available grazing permits. Note the direct correlation between profit and wild horse resource use: Every wild horse on the range costs ranchers approximately $216 a year—the difference between state and federal grazing lands.

The number of animals that can graze on the land depends on range conditions, which are variable depending on weather and other conditions. Cattle must be removed from the land in winter months, to allow the range to recover. Wild horses, however, graze throughout the year. If range conditions are diminished through this year-round grazing, the number of permits are presumably restricted.

Federal law requires BLM range managers to maintain the long-term health of the range on public lands.[6] The number of permits available to ranchers each year depends on range health, as assessed by public range managers. Accordingly, if range conditions are poor, range managers must reduce the amount of livestock, wild horses, or wildlife on the range. This leads to three options: increase the hunting permits for wildlife, remove wild horses from the range, or reduce the number of permits for cattle grazing.

The language of the act requires federal range managers to grant wild horses first-in-time access to public lands. Under this strict reading of the law, federal agents would only sell the surplus forage to cattle ranchers after all wild horses had their fill of forage. In the background, state game and fish departments would manage wildlife forage use through hunting permits, which control the population of deer and other species. This is not, however, the reality.

Removing wild horses from public land makes more grazing resources available to ranchers. Ranchers have successfully limited competition for forage by lobbying for a lower "appropriate management level" of wild horses allowed on the range. To limit competition for the forage that cattle would otherwise enjoy, ranchers argue that wild horses are overpopulous or not worthy of protection. Managers have publicly told stories of wild horses dying of starvation because of overpopulation, not mentioning that humans are fueling the lack of available forage by putting cattle on the land.

What happens when the government decides that there are too many wild horses on the range? The BLM adjusts the population level. Wild horses are then subject to "management programs" through which federal agencies round up herds using helicopters. Wild horses are held in captivity until being sold at auction. Adoption rates are down sharply; a recent auction in Wyoming reported only eight bidders registered for a sale offering eighty carefully trained wild horses.

Wild horses are clearly losing the battle for forage on public lands. Today, more wild horses live in captivity than roam on public lands. In 2006, cattle and sheep consumed twenty times the forage consumed by wild horses and burros on BLM land.[7] In 2016, the Wild Horse Advisory Board of the Bureau of Land Management suggested that the federal government should kill 45,000 wild horses in captivity.[8] Although this suggestion was ultimately overturned, it drew attention to the issue.

As with so many problems, the question becomes, what is the solution? What is the alternative? Historically, wild horses had open access to plants on public lands. Each wild horse could take only what it could consume, eliminating the incentive to directly overutilize the resource. Wild horses may indirectly overburden the range by overbreeding—producing a population that exceeds the number of animal units the range can support. Without human intervention, this problem would resolve itself through complex natural systems. Wild horse populations would be naturally managed through predators killing wild horses, wild horses lacking the nutrition to breed, part of the herd relocating to new rangeland, or wild horses dying of starvation. Thus, the natural system is self-regulating—nature generally prevents tragedy of the commons through complex, dynamic interactions within and between ecosystems.

Human intervention to manage component parts of ecosystems alters natural self-regulation, however. Ranchers and state governments in the American West have long reduced the natural predators of wild horses—creatures such as the mountain lion—because they also kill livestock. Through bounty programs and private hunters, the number of predators able to kill wild horses has decreased.[9] Moreover, fencing and development of historic grazing land has reduced wild horses' range, lessening the possibility for moving from poor range conditions. These examples are specific to the issue of wild horses, but it is notable that virtually all natural systems now incorporate some human management.

If wild horses had cognizable property rights to public lands, they would maintain first-in-time rights to forage on rangeland. Their populations would not be culled through government-sponsored management programs. Under such a regime, one can imagine that ranchers would be less enthusiastic about killing the natural predators of wild horses and livestock, such as wolves and mountain lions. Indeed, recognizing a property right for wild horses to public range lands would have the indirect consequence of lessening human management of public land. Ultimately, however, it would reduce the subsidy of underpriced grazing permits to ranchers, and, by extension, to Americans who consume beef.

Case Study 2: Outsourcing Thick-Billed Parrot Recovery to Mexico

Thick-billed parrots, one of two[10] parrots indigenous to the United States, have a striking physical appearance.[11] They are approximately fifteen inches long and bright green with yellow and red accents. Thick-billed parrots are garrulous, inquisitive, and relatively tame. They are monogamous and highly social with well-developed group behaviors. They nest in tree cavities created by other creatures and eat the seeds of pine trees. Thick-billed parrots can live for more than thirty years.[12]

This endangered species has centuries-old importance. Native Americans may have traded live thick-billed parrots, the remains of which were buried with human remains and artifacts.[13] Historical evidence suggests that thick-billed parrots and their "feathers were likely of ceremonial importance in some Mimbres communities by [about] A.D. 1000." Early Spanish explorers recorded Puebloan groups trading thick-billed parrot feathers and keeping the animals. In 1583, Spanish explorers led by Antonio de Espejo reported seeing parrots in Arizona.

Thick-billed parrots continued to be seen in Arizona throughout the early 1900s but were decimated by hunting and largely gone by the 1920s.[14] Rare but confirmed parrot sightings were reported in Arizona in 1938 and an unconfirmed sighting was reported in New Mexico in 1964.[15]

There are also ninety-five parrots held captive in United States Association of Zoos and Aquarium facilities today.[16] Thick-billed parrots continue to live in the Sierra Madre Occidental range of Mexico, with an estimated population of approximately two thousand. Habitat fragmentation, deforestation, and climate change are the primary challenges to parrot survival.

ENDANGERED SPECIES ACT PROTECTION

On June 3, 1970, the thick-billed parrot was listed as an endangered species under the Endangered Species Conservation Act. Domestic efforts to satisfy the objective of recovery included reintroduction, so in the 1980s and 1990s, captive-bred and wild populations were released into the wild.

Considerable controversy exists regarding why these efforts were ineffective. The US Fish and Wildlife Service (FWS) described the efforts as largely a failure, possibly due to undetectable diseases among captive-bred populations and predation by raptors. Conservation groups have suggested that wild-caught birds will stay in the area into which they are reintroduced, "with reasonable levels of survival." Although reintroduction efforts were ultimately unsuccessful, they did attract attention to the plight of the parrots.

The fate of the thick-billed parrot within the United States seemed stalled after the reintroduction attempts. Beginning in 2006, a group of nongovernmental organizations and agency officials from Mexico and the United States conducted a series of meetings focused on recovery of the parrot.

In 2009, the WildEarth Guardians sued the FWS, seeking an injunction because the agency had failed to create a recovery plan for the thick-billed parrot within two and a half years of its listing, as is the stated policy of the FWS. In December 2010, the parties settled the suit in an agreement that required the agency to evaluate the draft addendum to the Mexican recovery plan, including requirements for a recovery plan in the United States, by June 30, 2013.

On June 19, 2012, the FWS published a draft plan recovery addendum with notice-and-comment rule-making running through August 20, 2012. The plan was coauthored by the Arizona Game and Fish Department.

Notably, the parrot recovery plan addendum was the first recovery plan effort ever produced to adopt, in its entirety, the recovery plan of another nation. The FWS adopted Mexico's 2009 recovery plan for the parrot, *The Programa de Accion para la Conservacion de las Especies: Cotorras Serranas (Rhynchopsitta spp.)* (PACE) produced by Mexico's National Commission of Protected Areas. The 2013 recovery plan addendum supplements PACE with summarization, reference information, updated information, details about the US historical range, and new partnership information. It was prepared by a team of biologists from the United States with Mexican experts providing input.

The key features of the recovery plan include a deferral to Mexican conservation efforts with no committed domestic efforts to reintroduce the parrot. The plan estimates that the cost of a captive breeding and reintroduction program within the United States would cost $81 million over the next fifty years. In contrast, the cost of thick-billed parrot translocation within Mexico is estimated to cost $50,650, with total recovery costs of approximately $5.1 million. The plan is silent as to the level of financial support that US government entities and nongovernmental organizations have contributed to Mexico to fund recovery efforts for the parrot.

OPPOSITION TO OUTSOURCING

The FWS's abdication of responsibility for parrot recovery created considerable controversy. Critical comments offered during the notice and comment period fell into three categories of arguments: (1) that the agency was failing to uphold its statutory obligations under the Endangered Species Act by not focusing on domestic recovery efforts; (2) that Arizona may provide a better habitat for recovery than Mexico for a variety of political, environmental, and societal reasons; and (3) that reintroduction techniques had improved since earlier efforts and should thus be employed to encourage parrot recovery within the United States.

First, comments questioned the legality of the FWS relying on Mexican recovery efforts rather than attempting to recover the species within the United States. WildEarth Guardians, the conservation group that brought suit to force the recovery plan, stated the plan dodged issues by arguing that primary focus of recovery should be in Mexico.[17] Defenders of Wildlife advanced a statutory argument that failing to recover the species domestically would be at odds with Section 2(a)(3) of the Endangered Species Act, in which Congress noted that endangered species "are of esthetic, ecological, educational, historical, and scientific value to the Nation and its people."[18]

Second, comments raised practical concerns that leaving the fate of the parrot to Mexican recovery efforts was ill-advised because those efforts may fail.[19] Furthermore, designating parrot habitat in the United States was important to species recovery.[20] Several comments compared the challenges of recovery in Mexico with the relative strengths of recovery in the United States. These comments noted that significant portions of Arizona habitat remain in suitable condition while significant portions of Mexican range are already gone.[21] One commentator noted the parrot became extinct here because hunters shot it and that hunting regulations protecting the bird are in place now.[22] Another commentator cited a study showing that while Mexico has a history of "parrot smuggling, bribery, and lax enforcement of parrot conservation laws," the United States lacks such a history.[23] Commentators suggested designating Arizona habitat as critical habitat under the Endangered Species Act would be the most effective way to conserve the species.[24]

A representative writing on behalf of impoverished Mexico *ejido* (community-owned land) members mentioned in his comment the cooperative agreement through which *ejido* members received payment in exchange for conserving the Protected Area.[25] The agreement for this forest, which had already deteriorated considerably, was set to expire in 2013.[26] The representative was not optimistic about continued protection of the forest thereafter, noting that school children hoped to become logging operators when they grew up.[27]

Third, comments advocated for species reintroduction[28] and translocation[29] noting that reintroduction techniques have dramatically improved since the previous attempts to reintroduce thick-billed parrots.[30] Comments specifically argued that the initial reintroduction was flawed.[31] A witness to the 1994 release of thick-billed parrots lamented that the flock was doomed because their wings had to be repaired, they had blood drawn twelve hours before release, and they wore irritating tracking devices.[32] Commentators argued that new translocation techniques, such as use of nesting boxes, increase the likelihood of success,[33] and that eggs would hatch outside the breeding facility to lessen the risk of disease. These efforts could be coupled with behavioral training for young birds that mimics parent-raised hatchlings.[34]

THE POLITICAL ECONOMY

The political economy of species translocation suggests that translocation will systemically occur on low-value land to avoid conflicts inherent with bringing endangered species to high-value land.[35] The case study of the thick-billed parrot supports this account.

Southern Arizona is valuable land used for cattle grazing, a lucrative business that forms an identity for involved parties.[36] Landowners are well organized, with over twenty preexisting formal groups to represent cattle grazing interests.[37] Southern Arizona landowners have experience resisting the listing of endangered species[38] and designation of critical habitat.[39] Thus, the interest group of grazers has effectively signaled to the FWS that translocating wildlife into southern Arizona is a contentious, costly, and time-consuming process. Arizona landowners actively worked with state and federal officials to abdicate responsibility to restore the parrot to its historical Arizona habitat. The bird was instead maintained in low-value Mexican land populated by rural, poor residents.

Another facet to understanding the decision of the FWS in the thick-billed parrot plan is the role of the Arizona Department of Game and Fish. Although proud of translocation efforts that took place on public lands, Arizona state officials are skeptical of translocations in the southern portion of the state, particularly after controversial wolf translocations. Arizona Game and Fish officials supported restoration of thick-billed parrot populations in Mexico rather than in Arizona.

Arizona Game and Fish was eager to retain state control over wildlife management; the existence of a federally listed endangered species within the state frustrated this goal.[40] States have primary authority for regulating species that are not listed as threatened or endangered, but the federal government has long had responsibility for conservation of threatened or endangered species.[41] The FWS is required to cooperate with states[42] and frequently works with state officials, but there is no option to del-

egate authority to state officials, as there is under other environmental statutes.[43] State officials' opposition to translocation of
the parrot likely strengthened the federal officials' unwillingness
to undertake domestic recovery efforts. Instead, the agency provided scientific expertise and funding to attempt to recover the
parrot in lower-value land in Mexico.

The economically disadvantaged, rural Mexican villagers who
received responsibility for managing parrot habitat and recovery efforts did not have a seat at the table in the United States'
recovery planning efforts.[44] The chances of habitat destruction
seem high, given many villagers' aspirations of becoming loggers and rampant illegal drug cultivation taking place in parrot
habitat. If the habitat is diminished, the United States has no
formally defined role for stepping in to restart translocations. Nor
can the United States control Mexican environmental agencies'
monitoring or enforcement of habitat protections.

If left unchecked, the recovery efforts for several species will
likely shift toward lower-valued lands both domestically and
abroad. The outsourcing of the thick-billed parrot is likely not the
last time the United States and Mexico will cooperate. The Sky
Island region,[45] which is the US habitat for the thick-billed parrot,
is a biodiversity hot spot containing more than twenty threatened
and endangered species.[46] Arizona Department of Environmental Quality officials advocate using the cooperation between the
United States and Mexico vis-à-vis the thick-billed parrot as a
model for other species, including the jaguar.[47]

Importantly, the thick-billed parrot is one of several species
for whom the best chance at preservation is no longer in its current habitat. The desert tortoise is routinely shifted from private
lands to captive breeding facilities or on to public lands to make
way for development projects.[48] The FWS has concentrated recovery efforts of certain species, such as wolves, on federal public
lands to avoid controversy associated with those species. In one
dramatic example, Alaska Department of Fish and Game officials waiting in helicopters shot and killed an entire pack of
collared wolves as soon as they crossed the boundary between

federal and state public land.[49] These anecdotes provide evidence of a broader trend of not only shifting species to lower-value lands, but of sometimes failing to do necessary translocations altogether. A recent empirical overview of species translocations shows that more than half of all translocations simply do not occur.[50]

Outsourcing and failing to translocate species when necessary for their survival threatens not only individual species but also diminishes protections against habitat destruction. This exacerbates problems leading to ecosystem degradation and further extinctions. Divesting species of valuable land is both normatively undesirable and incongruent with the mandate contained in the statutory language, legislative history, and Supreme Court precedent for the Endangered Species Act. Despite this, the solution does not rest in agency action, judicial review, or statutory fixes by Congress. Instead, property-based solutions are best suited to address what is, at its core, the property-based issue of habitat expropriation.

Case Study 3: Traditional Ecological Knowledge and Scientific Management of Caribou

Caribou are large, wild animals that roam North America and Greenland. Although the same species as reindeer, caribou are not domesticated or herded.[51] They are, however, a crucial part of the Alaskan ecology.

Today, the Western Arctic Caribou Herd is the largest caribou herd in Alaska, with a peak size of 500,000 animals and a range of 157,000 square miles.[52] A typical annual migration begins in the winter ranges, which are on the southerly Seward Peninsula and the Nulato Hills. The animals migrate northward in April and reach the calving grounds in the Brooks Range in late May to June. After calving, the herd disperses throughout its habitat to seek relief from the relentless insects. It spreads across the northern portion of the range during the summer, then leaves the Brooks Range in September to head south.[53]

The Western Arctic Caribou Herd occupies a landscape that is a patchwork of ownership among federal, state, native, corporate, and private landholders.[54] Each landowner has an individual approach to wildlife management, sometimes conflicting with others. This assortment of land management agencies, public and private owners, and administrative/jurisdictional issues creates a plethora of habitat management issues—the paradigmatic concern of wildlife habitat spanning many land parcels, to which wildlife has no formal claims.

In 1970, the Western Arctic Caribou Herd numbered 243,000, but in 1976, it dropped to 75,000. The population collapse had devastating effects on rural Alaskan Native villages, which depended on herds as a primary food source. Alaska Department of Fish and Game (ADFG) officials grew concerned that the caribou herds were declining. They attempted to curb caribou harvest, and thus increase herd numbers, by imposing limits on how many animals hunters could harvest in a specified period of time. ADFG relied on imperfect survey methodologies and discounted the number of caribou seen by Alaskan Natives who lived on the land full-time. ADFG held a series of hearings on the problem and issued 3,000 permits to Alaskan Native communities. The department failed to notify or invite representatives from the Athabascan communities to the hearing and later refused to issue permits to overlooked communities. Long-standing distrust exacerbated the poor relationships between government officials and Alaskan Natives during a time of crisis.

SOCIOECOLOGICAL BACKDROP

Native communities have populated what is Alaska today since time immemorial. The indigenous worldview incorporated animals and people as equal. Russia colonized Alaska, and the United States later purchased it. Eventually, the US government began regulating wildlife in Alaska.

Alaskan Native hunting practices differed from those endorsed by state fish and game agencies within the continental

United States. Alaskan Native communities historically killed many animals in a single day according to age-old practice, consistent with the migratory patterns of the Western Arctic Caribou Herd. For example, hunters from some villages would station themselves by a river, then wait until the animals swam across the river to harvest them, to maximize the take.[55] Such hunting practices use traditional ecological knowledge, an oral history governing the human relationship with the natural world that has only recently been recognized as valid by Western scientists and courts.

Early American settlers in Alaska poorly understood and actively discouraged Alaskan Native hunting practices. In the 1900s, Alaskan game wardens used fines, arrests, and gun confiscation to punish traditional hunting practices. Such enforcement mechanisms bred distrust between Alaskan Native communities and department officials, which, along with differing perspectives on wildlife management and ethical hunting practices, persists into modern times.

Today, between forty and fifty remote villages of indigenous peoples reside in rural Alaska. Many rural interior villages have no road access. Residents and government officials must use airplanes, boats, snow machines, and dogsled teams to travel to more populated areas, which are hours away. They must fly in fuel to power these vital forms of transportation.[56] Treacherously cold weather makes travel difficult and dangerous.[57]

Food security is a primary concern. Modern inhabitants of rural villages continue to live a subsistence lifestyle during times of food scarcity, depending on hunted and harvested foods for the majority of their diet. Caribou is a primary food source. In the 1970s, people died of starvation because of herd collapse. This is not a problem confined to history. In 2009, CNN reported on the conditions of life in rural Alaska. The reporting noted that "2 pounds of cheese costs between $15 and $18, milk costs $10 a gallon, a 5-pound bag of apples costs $15, and a dozen eggs costs $22."[58] The article reported a father of five children who goes "days without food in his house."[59]

The high cost of food does not operate in isolation. Transportation and home heating are exceptionally expensive. It can cost nearly $1,500 per month to heat a home. One stakeholder notes: "The rural communities have to choose between heat/fuel and groceries."[60] Fuel is flown in bulk to communities to fuel snowmobiles, which are crucial for transportation and food gathering. Even where distribution lines exist, they are subject to failure in the extreme conditions. "If the power goes down and the whole community goes down, it is a scary scenario if the people need medications, food spoils, and there are no communications."[61] Similarly, aging infrastructure in villages for things like sewage lagoons and roads is a concern.

Federal law and policy consistently overlook the practical realities of rural and subsistence lifestyle. For example, the trust land title restricts bank loans, and the Uniting and Strengthening America by Providing Appropriate Tools Required to Intercept and Obstruct Terrorism Act of 2001 ("Patriot Act") requires a home owner to have a physical address to secure a bank loan; these laws result in a lack of credit availability. Loan and grant programs do not acknowledge traditional subsistence economies. State welfare law defines poverty with regard only to income, not the heightened cost of living in remote areas. Well-intentioned programs can backfire. One program focused on improving building standards, but it increased pricing and delayed the building of new homes.

Social, cultural, and traditional values are also at risk. Rural interior communities tend to be quite small and deeply rooted in traditional practices. Climate change effects and conflict over natural resources development are rapidly changing traditional ways of life. As elders die, traditional knowledge is lost. This social backdrop has led to generational divides among communities.

LEGAL FRAMEWORK FOR MANAGING CARIBOU

Against the backdrop of sharply different perspectives and a century of distrust, state and federal agencies in Alaska continue to manage wildlife on which the lives of some rural Alaskan Native communities depend. A series of laws enacted by Congress in the 1970s, such as the Alaskan National Interest Lands Conservation Act, embedded subsistence hunting rights for Alaskan Natives and nonnative rural Alaskans into federal law. The Subsistence Resource Commission manages these rights and reports to Federal Subsistence Regional Advisory Councils and the Federal Subsistence Board. Alaska maintains a parallel system, which centralizes authority in the Board of Game and Fish and incorporates a broader focus on nonnative users, including game hunters from other states or countries.

In the period after the caribou population collapse, a complex arrangement between Federal Subsistence Advisory Boards and the Alaskan Board of Game emerged to govern hunting and fishing regulations. Various stakeholders would argue before the State Board of Game, which was "not very productive" because the groups had different interests, essentially leaving management to the game boards.[62] The Western Arctic Caribou Herd subsequently became the largest herd in Alaska, peaking at roughly 500,000 caribou.

In 1994, ADFG hosted a three- to four-day workshop to determine objective ways to assess caribou harvest levels. After-hours and in the hallways between sessions, participants began to discuss creating a working group devoted to the issue. Collaborative strategies were in their infancy in Alaska. Some state employees were familiar with the concept from their experience engaging with Canadians, whom a former state wildlife biologist described as "a decade ahead of Alaskans in terms of working groups."[63]

A small group hammered out the concept and structure of the Western Arctic Caribou Herd Working Group (WACHWG), the focus of which was to have field biologists and users from the major interests come together. The group sought to connect researchers and those reliant on caribou to have an informal, nuts-and-bolts discussion about the population, with the goal of offering a unified set of recommendations to the Board of Game that would improve its decision making. Jim Dau, a founding member of WACHWG noted, "We never envisioned anything formal. We wanted it to be informal, because that's the way villages work, that's what people were comfortable with." The WACHWG intentionally did not have a chair, seeking to avoid hierarchy. It also met in various rural villages, which allowed local villagers to attend meetings.

For several years, a group of up to nine people would gather for a day in Kotzebue or another rural location to discuss whether and how to form a group. As the idea solidified, it found a receptive source in John Coady, the supervisor for Region 5 of the ADFG, who lived through the caribou population collapse debacle in the 1970s. Coady allocated a modest amount of the existing regional budget to convene meetings, assigned an employee to the collaboration, and, as Dau noted, "had enough moxie for people to take this seriously."

Early members of the collaboration were poignantly aware of the challenges involved in forming a credible group. Dau recalls:

> It was really tough early on. We were acutely aware of the problems with us picking and choosing representatives of the various user groups, indigenous people, guides, transporters, and industry. We realized that if we picked the representatives on the group, it would lose a lot of its credibility. Our hand-picked representatives would just be seen as people friendly to Fish and Game, which would undermine the group.[64]

The group eventually decided to include twenty voting chairs who were representative of the public. They recognized they could not give a seat at the table to every interest, so they began with the groups most dependent on the caribou and worked out from there. There were forty to fifty communities dependent on caribou, so the board adopted the advisory system developed by the state of Alaska many years before as a model to structure native subsistence users' representation.

During initial discussions on establishing some type of comanagement group, some Native Alaskan participants expressed their desire to have legal authority to promulgate regulations.[65]

They wanted to be equal partners with the state of Alaska and federal agencies in managing the caribou herd. Agency officials responded that comanagement was impossible; there was no way state or federal agencies could cede or share legal management authority with them or any other entity. Because of agencies' inability to share authority, two leaders of the Alaskan Native community users dropped out of the group.

There was also internal resistance within the agency. Some employees feared WACHWG could become too influential and undermine agency influence. Initially, some federal agencies were mildly supportive but did not have time or money to participate fully in the 1990s. Dau remembers that a US Fish and Wildlife Service manager "came to every meeting [with the attitude] 'We can't do this. We can't do this. There is no legal way to share authority. There is no way to do this.'"

Rather than risk the collapse of the budding group by taking on sensitive issues, the organizers initially focused on addressing small issues to build up trust. For the first five years, it avoided management issues altogether to avoid "rocking the boat." Instead, the focus was on facilitating an environment in which the group could build trust and find a "grudging" consensus over time. The caribou herd was large and growing during this period, so there was no real controversial management issue requiring WACHWG's attention.

WACHWG eventually created a subcommittee to draft a cooperative management plan, which was released in 2003 and continues to be periodically reviewed and updated. The current plan contains seven elements: Cooperation, Population Management, Habitat, Regulations, Reindeer, Knowledge, and Education.[66] The plan envisions all stakeholders, including state, federal, corporate, and private landowners and resource managers, working together to carry out the group's goals by developing cooperative agreements, sharing resources, and providing support in implementation.

Today, WACHWG is a collaboration between stakeholders interested in the long-term conservation of the Western Arctic

Caribou Herd, the ecosystem on which the herd is dependent, and the traditional and other uses thereof. Stakeholders include "subsistence users, other Alaskan hunters, reindeer herders, hunting guides, transporters, and conservationists," along with agency staff managers, natural resource managers, and biologists who act as consultants to the group.[67] All are knowledgeable about, interested in, and care for the management and conservation of the Western Arctic Caribou Herd.

The group holds a meeting once a year, allowing biologists to update stakeholders on the status of the health and population of the caribou, the range condition, and other matters affecting the herd. Meetings focus on management and information transfer, with people talking about the issues they observe with respect to caribou. A typical meeting might include a specialist presenting information on the impact of climate, transportation, or public land use planning, or elders addressing the group drawing on traditional ecological knowledge disseminated through the generations. There is a technical committee that meets a day prior to the meeting to discuss "nuts and bolts, biology and ecology," along with other subcommittees, which meet as needed throughout the year.[68]

Jim Dau notes that the organization has shifted away from the original conception of connecting field biologists with resource users and toward including agency staff members with little on-the-ground experience:

> Now, there may be 75–100 agency staff at the annual meetings, some administrators and some biologists—none of whom more than occasionally do field work on this caribou herd. It has become a must-attend annual meeting populated mostly by agency staff who have little direct involvement working with this caribou herd, except for administrative stuff.[69]

The informal tenor of early meetings became more structured over time: today, there is a chair, cochair, facilitator, and several note takers for each meeting.

WACHWG operates on an uncertain budget. It is not funded by the federal government in the same way that various marine mammal groups have been funded in recent decades (e.g., Alaska Eskimo Whaling Commission, Beluga Whale Committee, and Polar Bear Commission). Over the years, the group has attempted to solicit independent funding to make it autonomous from agencies and less vulnerable to budget shifts. It received a Challenge Grant from the US Fish and Wildlife Service, which lasted for two to three years. That was enough time to hire a director; however, the grant was not renewed. Funding has been a major impairment for the group, which could not cover staff time to prepare for meetings or absorb the cost of biannual meetings.

Although over a hundred people attend WACHWG meetings, a National Park Service biologist believes the "delicate balance between being unwieldy and everyone having a voice" is struck largely through having a facilitator and cochairs who are adept at moving the ball forward. The location shifted from a rotating schedule of rural villages to Anchorage to limit the expenses of agency officials attending. The working group has collaborated with different federal agencies to implement a cooperative management plan to effectuate cooperation among resource management agencies and all people who value and depend on the caribou.

Today, the group—and the caribou at the center of it—face challenging times. Between 2003 and 2011, the population of the Western Arctic Caribou Herd declined at an average rate of 4.6% annually. As of 2011, the population of the herd was recorded at 325,000.[70] The caribou were traditionally used primarily for subsistence, and today around 10,000 to 15,000 caribou each year are killed for that purpose. Additionally, nonresidents and nonlocals kill approximately 500 to 800 caribou each year in hunting expeditions. The *New York Times* recently reported that a controversial predator control regime implemented by the state—killing wolves, with the hope of increasing the number of caribou—failed.[71]

Additional concerns arise due to resource development and westward mining expansion from Prudhoe Bay into the National Petroleum Reserve-Alaska. Continued expansion would require a transportation corridor to be cut through the range of this herd. These activities likely would affect the herd's migration and distribution. Increased tourist aircraft overflight may stress the caribou prior to the winter months at a time when they should be gaining fat reserves.

The primary benefit of WACHWG is largely understood as building strong and trusting relationships among the members. Village residents feel more positively about agency officials who participate in the group. The structural design that facilitated that trust, however, is imperfect. Because many group members have served for many years, there is infrequent turnover, which reduces the potential for information sharing (when group members return to their villages to share what they have learned). The group also comes at a professional cost to the biologists who participate because it lessens the time they can spend in the field. WACHWG founder Jim Dau notes, "We invested tremendous time and energy to initially establish and later support this group, and we paid dearly in terms of internal political capital." Nevertheless, the two-decades-long collaboration built relationships among previous adversaries and developed trust long absent between Alaskan Native communities and agency officials.

PRIVILEGING VARIED PERSPECTIVES

Contrast the difficulties borne by the representatives of the Alaskan Native communities to those of other stakeholders in the Western Arctic Caribou Herd. Agency officials, representatives of extractive industries, state and local government officials, and employees of environmental nongovernmental organizations all receive their wages for attending meetings because it is part of their jobs. This allows these stakeholders to engage in careful, data-intensive decision-making. However, costs of time and travel can serve as a functional bar against the perspectives of stakeholders whose time and expenses are not well funded.

Stakeholders with lower incomes but strong interests in the land and resources at issue may be displaced by stakeholder collaborations, relative to less-intensive public participation processes, such as notice-and-comment periods. Collaboration disadvantages interested stakeholders with insufficient resources to express that interest through attending meetings, relative to attending a one-time listening session or participating in public comment periods.

One response to this concern may be that sufficiently motivated stakeholders will pool resources to fund representation in collaborations. This may be true for certain interests, as with sportsmen's groups who have organized to quite effectively represent hunting and fishing interests. It is also true with respect to representatives from Alaskan Native communities, whose deep reliance on caribou has driven long-term involvement in the collaboration through communities pooling resources to send representatives. However, this optimistic account fails to account for the social and economic costs borne by rural populations who cannot afford to participate, but also cannot afford not to. Although this discussion focuses on Alaskan Native communities, the issue of involving certain stakeholders in collaborations is a national issue.

APPLYING LESSONS TO AN ANIMAL PROPERTY
RIGHTS REGIME

The Western Arctic Caribou Herd stakeholder group represents humans asserting human interests with respect to federal wildlife management. Under an animal property rights regime, stakeholders would be obligated to represent wildlife interests instead. Interestingly, several of the key people at the table likely would be similar, including wildlife biologists and indigenous people. The tourism and commercial hunting interests likely would be absent. Wildlife conservation nongovernmental organizations would likely be present. How, then, would property rights change the analysis?

Animal property rights would make the group subject to external scrutiny to ensure the animals' best interests—at an ecosystem level—are considered. First, this would require broadening the analysis to a more holistic perspective, such as expanding analysis up and down the food chain. Further, the central inquiry would be on how to create a sustainable ecosystem for generations of many species operating in the area, rather than sustaining a caribou population for human consumption.

The standards to which the group would be responsible would also change. First, the process would operate under trust doctrine rather than the statutory Administrative Procedure Act. Second, the nationally (or internationally) certifying body of animal trusts would provide an additional layer of expertise and oversight to the project, providing nationalized inputs and best practices. Crucially, the model of collaborative, interdisciplinary decision-making among key stakeholders would remain.

Part IV

Analyzing the Potential
of Animal Property Ownership

9

Evaluating a Property-Based Approach to Biodiversity Preservation

Benefits to Animal Property Rights

Approaching animal welfare from a property rights perspective achieves partial gains associated with a human rights approach, while avoiding some of its practical difficulties. First, a property rights approach does not revolve around the argument that animals are morally or intellectually equivalent to humans. Thus, it sidesteps the burden of convincing judges, and society, that humans and animals are the same. Degrees of similarity between humans and animals matter greatly for issues of extending human rights. One must delve into deep and unknowable questions about what makes us human. Such inquiries matter relatively little for property ownership.

Second, ample precedent exists supporting animals as property owners. Legal institutions have long extended legal personhood for the sake of property interests to nonhumans, including corporations, real estate investment trusts, and even ships. Animals already have a limited capacity to own property. I consider formalizing and expanding existing rights. Property rights have been expanded several times to accommodate expanded definitions of who "counts" as a property owner. Society has survived each shift.

Third, this approach does not require redistribution of property. Under a regime extending human rights to animals, people would presumably lose the right to own animals at some point. In this sense, humans would be made worse off to benefit animals. A property rights approach does not diminish the existing rights of humans to own pets or livestock, hunt animals on their land, or eat meat. Instead, it increases the capacity of animals without reducing existing property allocations among humans. Humans can give property to animals but are not required to, thus increasing choice but not creating a burden. Admittedly, the approach may lead to retitling some public lands already devoted to wildlife purposes to animal ownership, representing a loss in the total amount of lands held by the American public. However, this would be subject to democratic processes and thus reflect the political will of elected officials who would, presumably, weigh the public good of wildlife against little-used human interest.

A property rights approach targets more and different animals than existing approaches. The human rights approach most benefits human-like primates or sea mammals, whereas the welfare approach tends to focus on livestock and domestic pets.[1] Sea creatures and wildlife—a broad group of species ranging from ants and bees to lions, whales, and oysters—are the key beneficiaries of the property rights approach. Domestic pets benefit, too, aided by inheritance laws that allow them to maintain their standard of living on their owners' death.

This point highlights a vital aspect of my argument. The property rights approach should not be understood as an alternative to welfare or human rights, but instead as a complementary legal strategy with related objectives.

Similarly, this approach reflects a middle ground toward the treatment of animals. It reflects society's high value for animals better than existing welfare law does. However, it avoids the somewhat radical endgame of extending human rights to animals. When commentators consider the long-term implications of the human rights approach, it is easy to dismiss it as too extreme. The result would be a massive change in social norms relating to animals; consequently, many have an instinct to quash the first steps down a path with an extreme end. The property rights approach, on the other hand, avoids this slippery slope: humans would retain the right to own pets, eat meat, or kill spiders.

SPECIES CONSERVATION

Vesting animals with property rights reduces the potential for habitat loss on retitled lands. Although lands could be bartered or sold, animal trustees would likely only do so for welfare-maximizing exchanges that would ultimately benefit animals, such as trading a small piece of land near an industrial core for an expansive landscape in a rural area. Of course, there is a concern that captured trustees might inappropriately divest animals of their land in exchange for money, which is why the administrative concerns of appropriate trustees operating against the legal backstop of judicial review are important.

A property rights approach would not eliminate other protections for animals, such as easements or the Endangered Species Act. Instead, it would equalize the playing field by allowing animal agents to respond directly to localized species concerns. One example of how this might play out concerns predatory species, such as wolves or mountain lions, which kill domestic livestock. At present, federal agencies do not pay compensation for ranchers' claims that predators ate their livestock. (Private groups sometimes compensate ranchers for livestock losses due to predator kills.) In a scenario where animals are property owners, ranchers could presumably bring nuisance claims against them, seeking compensation for stolen livestock.

Unlike medieval English trials against animals, in which animals physically appeared in court, my model avoids the courtroom circus through using human representatives for animal owners. Over time, a compensation system would likely develop, whereby animal property owners would use land in either revenue-generating ways compatible with wildlife uses or isolated, high-value purposes. The revenue could be used to develop a fund with fixed compensation for livestock.

A property rights approach also provides an opportunity to update our approach to species conservation. We have had forty years of learning about the benefits and detriments of the Endangered Species Act; the rights-based approach provides the opportunity to incorporate these lessons. For example, this approach sidesteps the binary distinction between protected (threatened/endangered/critical candidate) species and unprotected species and allows for conservation at an ecosystem level. Careful management of animal-owned lands is, of course, fundamental to the potential of an animal property rights regime to encourage species conservation. Exploitation and poor management could also leave animals worse off. Again, this proposal considers the basic idea and its implementation. Best practices for on-the-ground management, compliance systems, and accountability measures are vital but outside the scope of this book.

At a general level, the idea of animal property rights certainly holds potential for improving species conservation by explicitly acknowledging human and animal competition for natural resources on the same plot of land. This regime offers an opportunity to explicitly acknowledge that initial entitlements excluded customary animal interests, which inadvertently created human-wildlife conflicts. Incorporating an animal property rights regime provides the potential for mitigating these conflicts. However, it is ultimately the administration of the regime that would determine the success of rights expansion.

Vesting widespread property rights in animals would likely shift the locus of action from federal agencies to animal landowners. This approach revitalizes nuisance suits to address environmental harms. Historically, some forms of water and air pollution were governed through a nuisance regime, in which aggrieved landowners brought suit against offending neighbors.[2] In the 1970s, Congress enacted sweeping environmental legislation, which largely displaced common-law approaches to pollution control.[3] Over time, however, federal environmental legislation stalled. Congress has not passed major environmental legislation since the 1990s, leaving major issues, such as fracking and emissions causing climate change, in the hands of agency regulation.[4]

Agencies seemingly focus on complying with federal environmental statutes, not on adjudicating nuisance claims by nearby landowners. Animal owners could more proactively seek nuisance relief from adjacent landowners that pollute air or streams. As property owners, animals would be entitled to the use and enjoyment of their land free from neighbors' disturbances. With strong property rights, animal trustees would be incentivized to sue polluting neighbors, both public and private. Threat of nuisance lawsuits brought by animal property owners may spur neighboring landowners to invest in pollution-reducing activities. Animal ownership might displace the recent primacy of statutory law for addressing environmental issues. It could function to restore a common-law nuisance approach—sometimes called free market environmentalism—to correct environmental ills.

DISTRIBUTIONAL EFFECTS

The distributional effects of an animal property regime are initially small but may grow over time. Jeremy Bentham argued that even terribly unequal property distributions should not be disturbed to avoid reducing the general welfare-producing effects of stable property regimes on society.[5] This thought experiment operates around voluntary transfers to animals, not a system of redistribution through which property is forcibly taken. Indeed, this approach may function to strengthen the property rights of existing landowners by reducing uncompensated wildlife takings of human lands.

The more troubling effects center on those who do not own property. One can imagine an argument that transferring property rights to animals arguably disadvantages lower socioeconomic status Americans by reducing the potential wealth of land held by the American public, which might translate into public benefits. This is a real concern. Historically, rural communities near natural resources harvested by government agencies produced funding which benefited local schools.[6] As federal land management policies have shifted toward conservation and away from timber harvest, some of these revenues have decreased. Under an animal rights model, however, it may be sensible to incorporate local and state taxes on revenue generated from natural resources extracted from the land. This would counter a frequent complaint about federal land ownership in Western states, and may even make animals more desirable neighbors than, for example, the Bureau of Land Management or Forest Service.

The broader social justice question is why animals, instead of other groups excluded from initial land allocations, should receive land. First, it is worth observing that this book is devoted merely to the question of capacity to own land, which other groups, widely recognized as the product of historic discrimination, have.[7] Second, this article is agnostic on the appropriate amount of land that animals should be granted. Instead, it focuses on exploring the idea and its effects, not on proposing to designate a set number of acres as animal-owned. Animal rights advocates, naturalists, and conservationists would also likely suggest that the benefits realized through animal ownership, particularly with regard to preservation of undeveloped land and preservation of biodiversity, are a public good that benefits all humans.

LAND USE PATTERNS

Animal property ownership would likely shift land ownership patterns in sweeping ways. At present, land ownership patterns in the American West are largely reflective of the grid surveying system, which broke extensive landscapes, including mountains and forests, into little squares for the sake of easy legal administration. Superimposing a grid onto a landscape without regard to the scale at which the natural resources therein must be managed created a strange mismatch between the size of property parcels (small) and the economically and practically efficient scale for managing resources ranging from forests to wildfire (large).[8] A key disadvantage to the present land distribution pattern is that it creates patches of land preserved for landscape interposed with private, sometimes fenced or developed, land. As a result, species that depend on seasonal migration may find their access to northern or southern lands blocked, or gone altogether.

Animal owners could act collectively to barter and sell disparate landholdings in exchange for collective blocks of uninterrupted range. In a series of Coasean transfers, high-value human land uses, such as subdivisions, could occur in areas near cities, whereas animal owners could increase their acreage in rural, remote lands that have limited human usage. This idea would require careful consultation with biologists, who would inform the trustees of animal owners of the habitat needs of animals.

This consideration highlights a key aspect of wildlife land ownership. If described at an appropriate state or regional level, animal owners would command economies of scale with regard to their landholdings that would largely serve to correct the problem of parcels versus landscapes created by historic disposition policies, which existed prior to modern understanding of ecosystems. Similarly, land uses that restricted access of animal landowners to their property, such as construction of dams blocking fish access to native streams, would be governed through property law rather than an environmental statute.[9]

Considering Counterarguments

Some may argue that shifting endangered species to public and foreign lands is a necessary, even desirable, action to fuel economic progress and land development. Below, I outline these counterarguments to my proposal, but ultimately argue that diminishing wildlife habitat by failing to recognize animals' interests in land frustrates economic, ethical, distributional, and ecological aims.

ECONOMIC CONSIDERATIONS

One can imagine an economic argument that landowners excluding wildlife from private lands is a rational response to resource constraints. Certainly, not all landowners could forgo their own uses to provide wildlife habitat. Therefore, society must decide which uses to allow. In some cases, it would be difficult to share the burden equitably. Historic processes of expropriation are difficult to undo, as with the example of the thick-billed parrot. The parrot lives in Mexico today. It would be costly and time consuming to move the parrot, and the outcome of translocations is at best uncertain. Resources would be better allocated toward species more reflective of American national identity or appealing to conservation ideas.

Where, however, is the limiting principle of such an economic analysis? This line of reasoning deems it sound policy to shift animals to lower-value lands; it might even argue for creating zoo-like sanctuaries for animals that live in high-value areas so land could be exploited for higher-value uses. This is not a hypothetical; wildlife farming is practiced in several African countries, and American wildlife is increasingly pushed toward constrained habitats.

A few free-market economists have recently made a widespread push to popularize wildlife farming in Africa and canned hunting in Texas, arguing that privatizing endangered species leads to conservation goals.[10] Some argue conserving wildlife should take a backseat to more compelling concerns, such as health care or education. The Endangered Species Act, they argue, is a product of the time in which it was passed, and is no longer relevant amid today's national concerns.

"Economics is all that matters" arguments fail for a variety of reasons. Public sentiment toward wildlife is clear. Congress, courts, and the American public have expressly and repeatedly prioritized the conservation, preservation, and recovery of endangered species. That commitment remains firm, with amendments, opinions, and polls demonstrating a sustained commitment to species preservation over other, even economic, priorities.[11]

Accepting the premise that species can be restricted to less valuable land diminishes the intrinsic value of species and undermines our country's ecological values. Such reasoning commodifies the value of animal habitat rather than capturing the full value of a landscape or ecosystem. Private lands can and do provide important ecological functions. Discounting the extent to which private property serves as wildlife habitat is clearly detrimental to wildlife.

Shifting wildlife to lesser-valued lands also inflicts harm on the human population.[12] Environmental law scholar Martin Krieger once famously asked: "Why don't we replace our forests with plastic trees?"[13] Krieger was making the point that natural resources have values extending beyond mere economic calculus, a principle with which even the most strident cost-benefit advocates agree.[14]

Moreover, land development encourages subsequent polluting uses. It tends to diminish the existence of raw natural beauty and landscape. This is not to be read as antidevelopment, but instead as a thumb on the scale for pragmatism. Let's acknowledge that although our society rightfully values property rights, there exists tension between the fullest extension of those rights (i.e., do whatever you want on your own land) and the broader societal interests in clean air, clean water, and reduced emissions. For these and other reasons, rights to individual development have historically been subject to some bar that serves broader societal interests. A mixture of legal and moral arguments rejects the notion that we need to commodify endangered species and restrict their recovery because of the value of land.

NONWILDLIFE INTERESTS

One can imagine critiques of animal property rights from both animal welfare and animal rights advocates. (I say "imagine" because, in my experience, both camps have welcomed this proposal.)

Why waste resources to give animals property if we actually

care about avoiding cruel treatment? Property rights do not help chimpanzees locked in undersized cages or livestock killed inhumanely. My approach dramatically increases the species of animals available for protection and offers a pragmatic approach that does not preclude other rights' expansions. Animal law presently focuses on the treatment of caged primates, farm animals, and domestic pets. Consensus has formed around "animals deserving of rights" as being limited to "normal mammals above one year in age."[15] Large categories of important animals are excluded, ranging from kittens to condors, baby seals to insects, on which whole ecosystems rely. My approach broadens animal law to include wild animals and animals all along the so-called tree of life.

Further, affording a property right to animals has both dignity and practical benefits. Theorists have long recognized the need for an incremental approach; coming from the side may be a better form of rights expansion than moving forward against great resistance. Although the property rights approach does not radically change the status or treatment of animals beyond formally granting them the right to hold property, it will likely produce subtle long-term gains that will increase over time. Further, the legally recognized ability to own property creates autonomy and dignity.

LIKELIHOOD OF IMPLEMENTATION

Unlike many animal welfare and rights approaches, wildlife conservation is a bipartisan issue.[16] Congress has demonstrated surprising and consistent levels of support for wildlife over time, even during eras of varying degrees of political gridlock. Implementing an animal property regime may be the most politically viable path to improve the treatment of animals.

Much of animal rights work pits people against animals. A horse sues its abusive owner. A whale sues the aquarium that holds it. A chimpanzee sues the researchers who hold it captive. Animal property rights takes a synergistic, complementary approach. It broadens the pie to include animals, rather than creating a zero-sum game in which humans are pitted against them. Frankly, this collaborative posturing of the legal approach to animal property rights likely reflects its creator: my other works study how highly localized groups of people can produce solutions that are superior to formalized, empirical methods. I believe in the wisdoms of crowds, that every person has value, and that people are fundamentally good and care about wildlife. From this collaborative—some would say female—perspective on the cooperative aspects of law and governance flows a solution that is less about adversarial litigation and more about producing consensus for progress. And I believe consensus would be the likely result.

Republicans and Libertarians would likely appreciate the extent to which a property rights regime displaces statutory approaches to environmental law, shifting from agency regulation to free market environmentalism that is characterized by nuisance-based claims. This approach shifts the foci of environmental law from agencies to courts. Moreover, the regime could be structured to generate revenue in a way that would appeal to fiscal conservatives. Land, for example, might be sold to fund animal conservation efforts, which would diminish reliance on public funds to support conservation. To the extent animal property rights increased the habitat or availability of game populations, it might enjoy considerable support among hunters. Finally, this approach does not require redistribution of property or call for weaker property rights; in fact, it might strengthen existing property rights by reducing the need for environmental laws that diminish them.

Democrats would likely respond well to animal protections that accrue from ownership. An animal property rights approach expands the category of potential litigants with standing to bring nuisance lawsuits against polluters and government agencies. Democrats, beyond the core animal rights and conservation constituencies, might object because this approach diverges from other, more pressing social justice issues, like the issues of reparations for African Americans or tribal sovereignty for and expropriation of Native Americans.

Ranchers and mineral developers likely form the core opposition to this proposal. Wildlife land uses conflict perhaps most directly with grazing sheep or cattle on land because of the direct competition for grass. Ranchers have long received massive federal subsidies in the form of grazing permits on federal land that are underpriced relative to private and state permits. Attempts to limit the availability of such permits cause tremendous backlash from farmers, as illustrated through the Bundy and Hammond, Oregon, controversies, in which armed militiamen faced off with federal land managers to protest grazing limitations. Ranchers are physically protecting what they believe to be incursions on their property rights on behalf of wildlife. Law currently forces ranchers to internalize the costs of predatory animals near their lands, which breeds frustration and leads to intentional habitat disruption and the killing of predatory species. Transferring the admittedly imperfect present system to a market-based approach with compensation for animal takings of ranchers' chattel would benefit both ranchers and predatory species, and allow for more natural management of prey species like deer.

CONCERNS OF CAPTURE

"Capture" derives from the public choice notion that public officials are subject to interest group capture, in which ostensibly neutral figures in fact privilege a particular group over those they are supposed to serve.[17] Human representatives of animal landowners could be captured by a variety of interest groups: a particular species with a strong public following that advocates strongly on its behalf or humans with interest in animal-owned land, such as neighboring landowners. Human representatives of animal landowners would be particularly vulnerable to capture because their clients have zero capacity to monitor their behavior. Ants cannot, for example, file suit against a land manager who improperly manages their interests. Blackbirds cannot organize to ask for a new, more trustworthy trustee.

Moreover, protections against capture are scant. Human interest groups that might form to protect animal interests would likely be nongovernmental organizations, whose fundraising dollars disproportionately depend on charismatic species. Accordingly, the usual antidote to agency capture—outside litigation or lobbying—does not exist in this context. Seemingly the only protection would be whistle-blowing by insiders to the organization, a tenuous strategy worsened by the need for tremendous discretion to human representatives. Lest I overstate the risk of malfeasance, however, remember that the current system of public lands management is already subject to capture. It is not clear that animals would be worse off in a system in which their representatives were directly implicated in these decisions, rather than largess of landowners going to Congress.

Perhaps even more concerning is the potential for humans to use animal property owners for their own financial advantage. One can imagine adjacent landowners bribing human representatives of animal landowners to manage the land in a way advantageous to human interests by, for example, selling mineral rights or harvesting timber to reduce fuel loads and mitigate wildfire risk that might spread to nearby properties. Trust or fiduciary obligations, which are available under existing law, depending on the ownership model employed, would largely serve to mitigate such malfeasance.

Given the relative newness of formalized animal rights-holders, prophylactic legislation preventing abuse would be guesswork. Instead, the role of policing human representative behavior would fall largely to courts. In some ways, this is ideal: judges have experience applying trust law, assessing fiduciary duties, and policing the rights of those mentally incapable of legally representing themselves. Judges are not, however, experts in wildlife or land management. Yet they have made determinations on these issues for decades in the absence of statutory guidance.[18] To be sure, a lack of topic-specific expertise is not dispositive in finding courts ill-suited to make determinations; specialized courts and a system of special masters might emerge if necessary. Regardless, it seems inevitable that courts would play an active role in determining the fate of animal landownership.

Ultimately, there is reason for cautious optimism that existing legal institutions can accommodate animal landowners. Such institutions have long navigated property rights afforded to a variety of persons unable to represent their own interests, such as minors or the incapacitated. Moreover, the government is expert in handling the property rights of nonhumans, most notably corporations and other business structures.

10

The Implications of Interspecies Ownership on Property Theory

In chapter 1, I outlined the debate over how property rights emerge as a centuries-old debate within law. Relating scientific models of animal territoriality to property law may provide insight into this conversation. Vitally, this effort to connect science and law does not follow ugly historical attempts to use biology to distinguish among groups of people. It argues instead for the opposite: emphasizing the universality of property as a form of organization among all living things.

Comparing human property behavior with the study of animal territorial behavior sheds new insight into several core tenets of property theory. Broadly, once we situate property rights within the broader framework of nested systems of territoriality, it becomes clear that human property rules intersect bidirectionally with the property systems of other living things within an ecosystem. We may control ecosystems, but our social systems and governance mechanisms are also controlled by the environment in which they arise. Property law may be a human codification of a biologically driven need to operate under dynamic structures in order to achieve perpetual balance between resources and resource users.

Among animals, property rules and rights function as a natural, biological tool to prevent resource exhaustion. Individuals establish and defend property rights to secure adequate resources to survive and procreate. Property rights diminish the need to wake up each morning and fight to the death over where to eat and sleep. Instead, routine behaviors such as marking boundaries function as a proxy for physical altercation that might otherwise result when competing resource users enter the same territory. The time and energy saved can be invested in other activities, such as catching prey or creating iPhones.

A well-defined system of boundaries and fair shares of property likely contributes to social functioning, which again increases the survival of a species, as individual and as a whole, over time. Exclusion attained through boundaries, dispute resolution systems, and transfer rules allow survival. As a matter of natural selection, species that are good at establishing, defending, and maintaining rights will contribute their genetic material to subsequent generations—both as a function of having sufficient resources to breed and because they have not died trying to access those resources. Systems of property and related forms of governance are one mechanism to prevent resource exhaustion.

Rights likely operate as a nested system, occurring at a small level within individual members of a species and at a broader level across species.[1] Importantly, many scholarly accounts of how rights and norms emerge among humans are premised on direct connection to animal property behavior. Lobster fishermen,[2] whalers,[3] fur trappers,[4] tuna salesmen,[5] and cattle ranchers[6] are each responding to the patterns of underlying animal species.[7] The animals are in turn responding to the spatial and temporal distribution of the resources they require to live: prey, plants, shelter, and sunlight. Thus, human systems of property—and related social behaviors and governance—can be traced to the property behaviors of seemingly inconsequential features of the natural environments in which they live.

Amid resource exhaustion, resource users either move, die for lack of the resource, or kill one another. When demand outstrips supply, balance is restored through reducing the demand by reducing the number of resource users. This is true at the individual, ecosystem, and global level. Our system of property reflects the balance principle through nested mechanisms, both intentional (i.e., private systems of governing landscape-level resources, laws that do the same, interspersing communal and private landholdings) and unintentional (the way people diffuse over landscapes).

Thus, property rights exist to balance the demands of resource users (living things, including microbes, plants, and animals) against the supply of resources (e.g., sources of energy such as sunshine or food, water, shelter, and physical space). The emergence and dissipation of property rights are linked to resource abundance.

An individual or group will claim ownership over a physical space when the benefits of excluding others from that space exceed the costs. Costs will exceed benefits when the demand from potential resource users exceeds the supply of available resources. The spatial and temporal distribution of resources drives the size and shape of the parcel. Resource distribution, governance structure, existing social connections, and evolutionary propensities toward cooperation combine to determine whether ownership will be individual or communal.

Living things interact dynamically with their environment. The composition of the resource(s) used drives the social behaviors and governance strategies of resource users. Changes to the supply, demand, or distribution of resources in turn change the social behaviors and governance strategies of resource users. Such change may be slow or difficult to trace, however, because the process of natural selection endows the offspring of the best resource users with the traits necessary to manage the resource as it historically existed.

Property rights emerge and persist when resource demand is roughly in equilibrium with the supply of resources. When supply greatly exceeds demand, systems of rights loosen or dissolve because resource users can obtain adequate resources without the need to invest in defense costs. When demand greatly exceeds supply, systems of rights dissipate. This can lead to previously hostile groups sharing a resource because it is necessary to the survival of each. If a scarce resource is finite, animals will either leave the area or fight to the death to attain it. In this way, supply and demand are rebalanced. Importantly, resource abundance and the demands of resource users are in constant flux.

Rights as Determined by Resources

Under this account, factors affecting supply (the amount of resources) or demand (what resource users consume or want to consume) lead to adjustments in property rights. Crucially, however, this is driven by underlying natural resources instead of new market forces, such that the correlation between market forces and property rights have distracted scholars from the causal effects of resource systems on property rights. For example, property theorists have long identified new markets and new technologies as giving rise to property rights. Under the natural systems account the mechanism is not the new markets per se, but rather that they create resource tension where there was once abundance.

This observation sheds new light on Demsetz's anthropological case study. The Native Americans of the Labrador Peninsula used beavers individually when the resource was abundant. The emergence of a market created resource tension and the need for a system of property rights. Under the natural systems account, it was not the market per se that gave rise to the property right. It was the *effect* of the market on the balance between resources (supply) and resource users (demand). In other words, the market affected the number of beavers that Native Americans were attempting to trap, throwing out of balance the previously stable equilibrium of rights. This is a subtle distinction, but an important one—instead of some invisible hand rebalancing supply and demand, we see instead the need for balance in the underlying resources (beaver) driving the behavior of the resource users (hunters).

In conditions of resource abundance, in which the amount of resources exceeds the resource needs of potential users, rights will remain undefined. The cost of defining rights is an unnecessary expense relative to the low search cost of finding resources. If Bird 1 is eating from one flower, but a dozen more flowers are available, Bird 2 will merely fly to the next available flower. This appears to be true for humans as well. For example, if a recreational drone pilot is dominating one area of the sky, others will simply move away to other, available airspace.

Property rights emerge in conditions of resource tension, in which the number of resources is less than the number of users in a defined physical space but sufficient to support some resource users. Under such conditions, resource users will assert ownership over an area with sufficient resources to meet their needs. The size of the owned area depends on the underlying resource areas. In resource-dense areas, the owned area may be small. When resources are distributed in a patchy manner across the landscape, the territory will be larger. Animals are constrained from claiming areas that are too large because defense costs eventually become too great.

When a resource must be managed at a scale greater than individuals can effectively defend, groups will cooperate to manage the resource. Resource users may collectively assert ownership to an area, creating a communal ownership regime. Within the group area, group members may act communally to use resources as a group, without delineating individual rights. Alternatively, the group may defend some rights communally and allow individual ownership within the broader space. Among animals, wolves manage prey resources in a limited-access commons and maintain individual den spaces for breeding within the common space. Among humans, foresters manage pests, wildfires, and some hunting rights collectively while maintaining individual landholdings for timber operations. In every human society, effectively managing a landscape requires a mix of individualistic and collective use. Thus, the division between individual and communal rights is basically a false dichotomy—a point to which I will soon return.

Under conditions of extreme resource scarcity, in which the number of resource users dramatically exceeds the amount of available resources, respect for property rights devolves. The species reverts to either the evolutionarily disadvantaged tactic of fights-to-the-death over resources or to a situation in which usually warring groups cooperate. Macdonald and Johnson discuss this behavior as common between humans and animals with respect to limited water. Drawing on a variety of sources, they note that usually hostile baboon groups do not fight when the water availability is reduced to a single waterhole. Similarly, distinct or even warring human groups cooperatively share water during times of scarcity. This holds true, however, only as long as the resource is sufficient to supply both groups. If supply is sharply limited, groups may fight to control it.

People and animals alike act cooperatively to create synergistic use of land and resources with advantages over individual use. Resource mixes appear that maximize the resources relative to the needs of the resource users. For example, people manage water resources for a variety of drinking, agricultural, and environmental purposes. Many public lands are managed to balance various uses and objectives. In addition to the resource mix—a description of which resources are being used—so too are there governance mixes. Whereas property scholars once described a system of "private property" in the United States, this is an oversimplification of how ecosystems are actually owned. In practice, various component parts can be owned privately but also be collective, communal, public, or unowned. Ownership mixes are subject to attendant governance mixes, with public and private coordination of resource use occurring at various levels. Property is far messier than legal casebooks might suggest. As a construct describing complex adaptive systems, property usages, ownership, and governance must have the flexibility and nestedness of the underlying systems being governed.

Stateless Property

Adam Smith assumed that property and government were interdependent. This has proven a persistent idea. Douglass North, a

Nobel Prize–winning economist, noted that "a theory of property rights and of their creation is certainly incomplete without a theory of the state."[8] The biological basis of the natural systems account throws doubt on these observations. The statelessness of animal property rights is one of its distinctive features. Among animals, one clearly observes property without government—birds are not wearing curled wigs and black robes, and there is no apparent courthouse among chimpanzees. But animals clearly have governance—self-enforcing social rules that maintain social structure. Thus, the natural systems account might suggest rephrasing Smith's account to say "property and governance [as opposed to government] are interdependent." With this slight reformulation, his finding would apparently hold for creatures other than humans.

Rephrased as such, Smith's work sheds light on an important, underexplored aspect of animal property. The resource distribution hypothesis supports the notion that group existence—and thus emergent social behaviors, norms, and enforcement mechanisms—is linked to the resources the group is jointly exploiting. This may explain why so many governance mechanisms studied in law are tied to groups of resource users who develop communal rules to manage a defined physical space. Differing geophysical, geological, and climatic conditions can produce differing rules on ostensibly the same governance question.

Smith believed that government existed mostly to safeguard property ownership. Cooperation among resource users protects property and manages resources in an economically efficient way—not only to prevent exhaustion but also to communally manage landscape-level assets and threats to maximize the value of individual landholdings. The work of Ellickson and Ostrom supports this. Their study of governance of natural resources—bottom-up norms enforced by groups—parallels the cooperative nature of some animal property behaviors.

The link between human and animal norms suggests that perhaps property law is merely a codification of the rules that naturally develop in response to specific landscape conditions. This may explain several features of our property law system, such as why land uses are governed at the local level under a federal system. It also explains why there are different property laws in different areas of the country: laws governing water and oil in Texas are almost entirely different than those in Pennsylvania. The reasons for those differences are clear if we believe that property rules are responsive to local resource conditions.

The False Dichotomy of Communal and Individual Rights

Perhaps the most interesting modern scholarly debate about property is whether it is fundamentally exclusionary[9] or inclusive[10] in nature. Property law tends to attribute the composition of a right to political or social factors. Addressing this debate from the perspective of animals transforms it into a biological observation rather than a normative prescription. In fact, the division between communal/private and exclusive/inclusive rights seem artificial under a natural systems account: property rights must be at once individual and communal, inclusive and exclusionary. Animals and humans alike divide land into a mix of private, limited-access commons, open-access commons, and unowned spaces. Biologists accept that the scale and richness of underlying resource(s) determine the form of the right.

It is nonsensical to look at any property right in isolation—say the right of the farmer to till her land. Only in theory can this right operate in a vacuum. In reality, it is inexorably intertwined with overlapping resources and pollutants that must be managed in order for the farmer to farm. Some resources and pollutants can only be managed at a much larger level than that of an individual landowner, because that management requires limited-access commons or public rights. For example, the farmer is unable to manage her land absent pest control, water irrigation, and airspace rights. Administrative commons are similarly necessary: in a world without social norms, contract, and government, she may not have the ability to exclude others from her farm for the duration necessary for her seeds to yield crops.

Every landscape is comprised of many overlapping virtual parcels with different scales of management. Land parcels divide landscape-level resources into small pieces, which must be re-assembled in order to effectively manage large-scale landscapes. Individual landowners must collaborate to maximize the value of their individual resources that operate at a scale beyond the individual parcel. Resource users can assemble virtual parcels—boundaries around resources that differ from the linked parcels of land. Custom, law, and public lands are basically interchangeable in serving to piece together fragmented resource parcels. Animal behavior supports this nascent economic argument that all property must at once be individual and collaborative. For a property user to maximize one resource managed at an individual level, she must cooperate with surrounding rights-holders to manage other resources that operate at a scale that requires collaborative management.

Below, I highlight examples from animal and human behavior illustrating this point. I begin with animal examples, then move to human illustrations.

Lions always maintain territories with two watering holes.[11] If they have a single watering hole, they will overhunt it and exhaust the prey resources. With more than two watering holes, the cost of defending the territory becomes too great. With two watering holes, the pride rotates kills of herbivore prey. The distance between the two watering holes is a strong determinant of the size of the lion home range. If prey are abundant at nearby watering holes, the territory is small. When the watering holes—and associated prey—are spread out, the lion pride maintains a larger territorial size. The lions must cooperate. No single lion can maintain a territory size large enough to sustain two watering holes. The number of lions in the pride is a result of the distance between the two watering holes.

Among humans, private foresters paradoxically complained when their largest competitor—the US Forest Service—stopped logging national forests. This result is largely inexplicable under standard property rights theory coupled with economic analysis: decrease in supply by the largest landholder would ostensibly be a boon for smaller, private timber operators. In fact, foresters were responding to the fact that to maximize their individual rights to harvest timber they had to cooperate to manage the larger-scale considerations of both forest fire and production sufficient to sustain timber mills. Antitrust laws prevent foresters from cooperating on issues of pricing, but as a matter of necessity they must pool some resources to maximize their individual parcels.

Similarly, cattle grazing was not a profitable venture in the American Southwest until ranchers organized predator abatement.[12] Under natural conditions, indigenous apex predators, such as mountain lions or wolves, would kill the cattle released onto large, open landscapes to graze. The patchy resource distribution of range grasses meant that cattle had to stray far from one another, making protection by humans or dogs infeasible. Unabated, kills would reduce the cattle that could go on the market and thus reduce profits. Yet no single rancher could unilaterally protect his property from the predators, the habitat of which spanned many ranches. Thus individual cattle ranchers cooperatively funded bounty hunters, who would eliminate predators from the desert landscape. Cattle ranching became profitable by cooperatively managing the landscape-level resource of natural predators. Ranchers lobbied state officials to provide predation reduction services—which many state wildlife offices continue to provide today.

The collaboration necessary to manage large-scale resources contributes to social and governance structures. For example, Alaskan Native communities' social structure, including local government, is premised on the need to cooperate for whaling. Unlike many other animals, whales cannot be hunted by an individual.[13] An Iñupiaq whaling captain describes how the need for this large resource necessitates social cooperation:

> The whale being the center of our culture, it was the one animal that no one person can catch on their own, unlike any other animal or mammal where folks can catch alone. It took cooperation; it took teamwork. It brought people together . . .[14]

Entire social structures are built around whaling; the captain of the whaling boat is also the community leader. All members of the community work collectively to successfully whale. When a whale is killed, the captain distributes the meat according to formal rules, which are passed down from captain to captain.

The need for collaboration to produce individual property extends beyond real property. To incorporate a female-lead example, my great-great-grandmother's Milbank, South Dakota, community was structured around quilting bees. Quilts were a vital component of daily life: used for bedding, as doors, and even as currency.[15] But no single woman could make a quilt alone. Instead women sewed quilt squares individually, at home. But the process of assembling the individual squares required many women to work together at once to quilt the tops. A group of women rotated from home to home for "quilting bees." Each woman's ability to produce a valuable quilt was dependent on her inclusion in an ongoing social group. The social group, according to my grandmother, was the cornerstone of Milbank life. Similar dynamics explain technology products that result from patent pooling,[16] or even the accretion of knowledge necessary to create scholarly theory.[17]

Having set forward a handful of examples, I will return now to the broader point: all systems of property rights are necessarily comprised of many rights simultaneously operating at different levels. The reasons for a species choosing one over another is a mix between the evolutionary skill set of the species and the underlying resource conditions (e.g., spatial distribution, scarcity). Ants, for example, have a remarkably sophisticated system of property, which has evolved over millions of years. Members of that species are so evolved toward a communalistic system that they could not survive individually. Species success requires flexibility in adapting systems of rights to changed resource conditions.

Conclusion: Are Animal Property Rights the Rights of Nature?

At the beginning of this book, I suggested that my proposal speaks to the rights of nature movement. Yet the wildlife at the heart of it are merely a synecdoche for nature. In my framing, "animal property rights" are essentially animals as rights-holders to ecosystems. A parallel framing of animal property rights is as ecosystem property rights, particularly when one considers the three primary bases for extending rights: a biological mandate, customary practice, and scientific description of animals as active participants in our system of property with similar property behaviors. Each of these underlying rationales extends equally to plants, bacteria, and ecosystems.

This book hints at a broader proposition: Perhaps *all* living things use communication, coordination, and conflict to balance resources to resource users among and between species. I overview recent research in microbiology, plant biology, and oceanography that suggests territoriality exists in each of these domains.[1] These fields are relatively new: the data are less complete than in the robust field of animal territoriality. Overviewing the findings collectively suggests the possibility that all living things demonstrate behaviors designed to provide ecosystem-level balance through cooperative management of common-pool resources.

This contributes to my conception of the "natural system account" as both a complex system and a nested system.

Plant Territoriality

In 1999, biologists H. J. Schenk, R. M. Callaway, and B. E. Mahall wrote an article suggesting plants exhibited territorial behavior of defense and exclusive use of space.[2] Scientists have since published hundreds of articles and several books on the topic. Here I review the findings of the original article and subsequent literature.

Plants exhibit defense and exclusive use of space through root segregation. Each plant has roots extending underground into the soil. The roots of plants growing in isolation are more widespread than plants growing adjacent to members of the same species ("conspecifics"), a phenomenon known as root segregation, an interaction between the plants to avoid the roots of competing species. Such segregation occurs in scales ranging from meters for whole-root systems to millimeters among individual roots.

In 1946, Cornelius H. Miller diagrammed two neighboring plants of *Parthenium argentatum* (guayule) seeded in Salinas Valley, California, into Greenfield loam (soil). There were no neighboring plants on either side. The root systems spread laterally toward unoccupied soil, but there was limited growth between the plants.[3] Headley and Alkadry provided this as an example of the extent to which plants avoid roots of neighboring plants.

Plant biologists have observed similar root segregation among apple trees, peach trees, soybeans, and onions. In one example, an apple tree growing in isolation has a widespread root system. When apple trees are planted near one another, the root systems vary from the isolated example, showing less horizontal overlap than would be expected from mere extrapolation of the isolated species. Similarly, peach trees avoid the roots of adjacent peach trees almost entirely.

Plants growing in natural ecosystems display greater segregation than would be predicted by a null model of symmetrical root distribution. A quantitative study of *Lareira, Liquidambar,* and *P. taeda* showed that plants growing in isolation had symmetrical horizontal root distribution, whereas plants growing next to conspecifics had little horizontal overlap. Root segregation also occurs between species ("intraspecies"). In natural and laboratory settings, the root systems of shrub species inhibit the root system of another, nearby plant of a different species. For example, the root system of the shrub *P. spicata* decreased after coming into contact with the roots of *A. desertoum*.

Plants rely on five mechanisms to exclude the roots of other plants: resource depletion, exuding toxins, sending chemical signals, sending electrical signals, and soilborne diseases.[4] Sometimes the leaves, stems, flowers, fruits, and seeds produce substances that leach into the soil and deter competing plants. Such is the case with *Juglans nigra* (black walnut) trees, which emit juglone, a quinone, through roots and leaves. Apple trees release glycoside, a phlorizin, through root bark, which inhibits root growth of bioassays. The *Grevillea robusta* tree produces a compound in roots that kills conspecific seedlings when their roots come into contact with mature trees—a tree equivalent to infanticide. Plants also emit chemical signals, which are hypothesized to communicate between plants and competitors. Similarly, roots generate ionic currents—electrical signals—to signal to other plants.

One explanation for root segregation rests in resource depletion. If one species depletes the soil's resources, other roots likely will not extend into the depleted soil. For example, some deciduous trees exclude other species from growing in their understories by reducing water resources to a degree below other species' tolerance level. Scientists also suggest that territoriality among plants is linked to evolutionary fitness. Among desert shrubs, the species with the highest degree of territoriality uses water most efficiently. Territoriality increases when plants have limited soil, light, and nutrient resources.

Sociomicrobiology

At least one scientist suggests the origin of territoriality began with microbes. R. J. Wolfe noted, "Territoriality, one of the fundamental principles of ecology. Microbes did it first."[5] This observation derives from the emerging field of sociomicrobiology, which focuses on the cooperative behaviors, communication, and territoriality of microbes.

In 2011, a groundbreaking paper showed territorial behavior among bacteria, using the example of *Proteus*.[6] *Proteus* is a bacterium found in soil, contaminated water, and the intestinal tract of animals. In people, *Proteus* can cause infections in the urinary tract, ears, nose, throat, and skin. *Proteus* migrates through a pattern called "swarming," in which swimmer cells transform into swarmer cells, which move across the surface of a liquid in coordinated movements. Cell colonies among the same isolate (sample) merge when they meet. However, when two different colonies from two patients meet, the strains avoid one another. Louis Dienes first observed in 1946 that both colonies expand in other directions while avoiding physical contact with the other colony. A boundary, visible to the naked eye and ranging from 0.5 to 3.0 mm, forms between the two colonies. This boundary is called a Dienes line.

Scientists have recently described this boundary formation as a "vivid example" of territoriality in bacteria, noting that "one strain is able to hold off and inhibit colonization by a competing different strain. It is an act of mutual exclusion."[7] One theory regarding the mechanism by which cells create the boundary is that swarming *Proteus* cells secrete toxins that kill other strains of *Proteus*.[8] Under this theory, the boundary between strains is comprised of dead cells that were killed by the toxins of the competing strain. Another theory, however, suggests that swarms recognize the competing swarms as such and signal the other through cell-to-cell contact.

Regardless of the mechanism, the authors noted: "In boundary formation, there is not only social recognition but also territorial competition between approaching *Proteus* strains." *Proteus* is not the only bacteria that exhibits territorial behavior. *Escherichia coli* and *Myxoccocus xanthus* operate similarly.[9] In addition, "*P. mirabilis* swarms are capable of territoriality and self- versus nonself-recognition."[10]

If we accept the essential roles of microbes in our evolution and existence, should they be afforded some rights? After all, I assume we are concerned about protecting all living things, except, of course, malicious creatures like mosquitoes. Bacteria are essential to the life of every eukaryotic organism on Earth; without bacteria, we would have defective immune systems, malfunctioning digestive systems, and no plants or flowers. The bacterial denizens of humans are certainly not new players, but only recently has science demonstrated their critical roles.

Interestingly, granting rights to microbes is a proposal that has already ocurred. In 2004, Charles Cockell proposed that microbial communities and ecosystems should be protected. He argued that since microbes enable all other life forms, they should have some constitutional rights.[11]

Ecosystems

Research about ecosystems suggests they similarly operate around resource distribution. New research suggests that evolutionary models of individual competition may be incorrect. Instead, scientists have observed within ocean ecosystems an evolutionary dynamic that increases resources for the whole system, "so everyone is better off. It increases total system resources."[12] In other words, groups of species evolve, relying on ideas such as cooperation, in addition to the evolution of individual members of a species. Researchers suggest this is a nested system that operates at different scales throughout the biosphere. If correct, these insights might reshape the way we think about property rights management and suggest an alternative to the resource competition model, encouraging a shift to see both the inclusive elements of property (in addition to the exclusion focus). Indeed, these findings might extend beyond the theoretical and open the door to ways in which cooperative behavior might influence human resource use.

As this discussion suggests, there is no reason that "animal property rights" should be distinguished from "ecosystem property rights." Although the bulk of this book focuses on animals as a more familiar—and frankly sympathetic—placeholder for ecosystems, the functional result is the same. I am supportive of natural property rights and see mine as a variation and legal framework within the broader concept.

Preexisting Natural Rights

Much like animal property interests, there also exists a strong case for the proposition that ecosystem property interests already exist. First, existing laws protect ecosystems in a variety of ways that resemble rights-to-nature proposals. For example, the Endangered Species Act applies to plants, and the National Environmental Policy Act requires agency decisions to explore the effect of government on several elements of an ecosystem. Natural resources damages require parties that spill oil or chemicals into waterways to restore the plant and animal systems.

Also, it is inaccurate to suggest that governments *could* grant a right to nature; many indigenous governments have always explicitly granted robust rights to nature. Much like suggesting that animals have customary rights based on precolonial laws, so too might ecosystems have customary rights. Indigenous peoples in North America had elaborate, well-formed systems of government before colonization. To state the obvious, many indigenous peoples in the United States *still* have sovereign governments with constitutions, judiciaries, executives, agencies, and legislatures. Many tribal governments recognize natural property rights.

In the influential book *The Rights of Nature*, David Boyd rightly situates innovations in the United States regarding natural property rights as part of a growing international movement. For example, the Navajo Nation Code—roughly equivalent to the US Constitution—states:

> All creation, from Mother Earth and Father Sky to the animals, those who live in the water, those who fly and plant life have their own laws and rights and freedom to exist.[13]

The constitution of the Ho-Chunk Nation states:

> Ecosystems, natural communities, and species within the Ho-Chunk territory possess inherent, fundamental, and inalienable rights to naturally exist, flourish, regenerate, and evolve.[14]

Crucially, indigenous peoples are everywhere leading the charge in natural property rights, by merely formalizing and expressing rights that have always been part of their laws and government. I suggest that precolonial property rights persist under customary law unless treaties explicitly extinguished them.

Ecosystems, animals, and nature have latent rights which have lain dormant but still exist. In other words, people need not ask legislatures or courts to give nature rights. Instead, social entrepreneurs merely need to mobilize institutions to begin leveraging those rights to protect nature. This bottom-up approach encourages many small efforts to collectively protect ecosystems at a local level, with trickle-up effects that will create societal change.

Property Rights for Inanimate Things

Rights expansion may prove to be a slippery slope. Should property rights be extended to all living things, including plants? To all natural things, such as rivers and mountains? What about computers? Microbiomes, which also organize and collaborate? Perhaps the definition presented in this book is already overly broad. One can imagine distinctions between wildlife and domestic animals, which the law already recognizes. A philosophical approach might distinguish different levels of animals based on capacity for pain or intelligence, with primates, but not insects, receiving property rights.[15] This discussion in some ways mirrors questions of standing, in which courts have considered the idea that trees, rivers, or wind may have the ability to bring a legal claim.[16]

My articulation for a "correct" limiting principle for distinctions between animals and other things potentially worthy of property rights depends on biology, common-law property principles, and biological information. For over one hundred years, Congress has afforded special attention to wildlife, embedding quasi–property rights to wildlife through the Organic Act of the National Park Service,[17] the creation of national monuments and wildlife refuges, and in affording wildlife what essentially serve as easements under critical habitat designations under the Endangered Species Act. Similarly, at least one articulation of Native American conceptions of property distinguishes "children, beasts, birds, fish and all men" as the owners and users of "woods, the streams. . . ."[18] In this sense, I am not so much forging new ground through a property rights regime but rather unifying existing law and public preference in a more formal recognition of animal property rights.

Should governmental action and human preference coalesce in the future—or if someone can convincingly argue that it already has—around plants or mountains, I see no reason the property rights approach could not extend to these things as well. Property rights have expanded numerous times in the past; there is nothing to suggest they cannot continue to expand or contract over time. (I do, however, draw the line at biology; my analysis does not extend to artificial intelligence or computers. It would not even include ships or corporations.)

The property rights approach to animal welfare sidesteps the difficult question Richard Posner raises regarding where animal rights end under the human rights approach, namely where the revolution ends. Americans lost the argument that property is inherently human when we afforded it to inanimate forms, such as corporations and trusts. Although one can argue such instruments indirectly serve human purposes, there exists no bright line between human and nonhuman with regard to property rights. This is one sense in which the property rights approach to welfare is an easier path than the human rights approach; we are dealing with a line that has already been redrawn to be more expansive. Extending it a bit further to formally include animals is not much of a leap legally. Yet animal property rights hold tremendous promise for reintegrating natural interests into human institutions.

Acknowledgments

I dedicate this book to my daughter Camellia, with love. Camellia's birth transformed my work on environmental issues from a profession into a passion. Her early childhood is inexorably intertwined with this book. Witnessing Camellia's early love for wildlife, plants, landscapes, and rocks reminded me of the innateness of our human need to connect with nature, of treating other inhabitants of this planet in a fair and moral way.

Christie Henry was a tremendous early supporter of this project; she has since become a wonderful friend and mentor. I am also grateful to Scott Gast, Rachel Kelly Unger, Nicholas Lilly, and Susan Olin for their help and support in bringing this book to fruition.

Scholarly communities within law, philosophy, and ethology have greeted the idea of linking property law with animal territoriality with generous enthusiasm. Several scholars provided outstanding feedback, including Irus Baverman, Julien Betaille, Eric Biber, Guillaume Chapron, Jason Czarnezki, Bob Ellickson, David Farve, Lee Anne Fennell, John Hadley, Bert Hoelldobler, James Krier, Justin Marceau, Ben Minteer, Martha Nussbaum, Con Scholobokoff, Ilya Somin, Jeffrey Stake, Kristen Stilt, and Annecos Wiserman. More broadly, scholars within the fields of environmental, natural resources, and animal law have provided unflagging support of my work in this and other topics. For this, I am thankful to Vanessa Casado-Perez, Jane Cohen, James Coleman, Robin Craig, Monika Ehrman, Bruce Huber, Bryan Leonard, Dean Lueck, Gary Marchant, and John Nagle. I am deeply thankful for the helpful feedback provided by over ten anonymous peer reviewers throughout the publication process; this book is better because of them.

My legal mentors and friends have had a tremendous impact on my work and life: Lisa Bernstein, Richard Epstein, Judge Jolly, Brian Leiter, Saul Levmore, Jonathan Masur, Martha Nussbaum, Omri Ben Shahar, Geoff Stone, and Lior Strahelivitz. Generous colleagues at Arizona State University have supported me in innumerable ways; I am especially grateful for the friendship of Angela Banks, Dan Bodansky, Adam Chodorow, Laura Coordes, Betsy Gray, Zack Gubler, Zachary Kramer, Rhett Larson, Gary Marchant, Troy Rule, Victoria Sahani, Erin Scharff, Josh Sellers, Mary Sigler, Judy Stinson, and Douglas Sylvester. My early teachers laid a foundation for me to lead a happy, productive life, particularly Diane Brickell, Daniel Bringle, Ernie Michelli, and David Robinson.

Law students have invested time and support in the ideas in this book from their earliest inception. I am thankful for the excellent research assistance performed by Casey Clowes, Dana Evans, Challie Facemire, Andrea Gass, Hayden Hilliard, Tessa Hustead, Daniel Kolomitz, and Jamie Lee. Christopher Johnson's visionary embrace of combining law and ethology inspired other editors at the *University of Colorado Law Review* to publish the first article about animal property rights in a legal journal, laying the foundation for the idea within the United States legal system. Several sections of this book originally appeared in law review articles, including *Harvard Environmental Law Review*, volume 43; *University of Colorado Law Review*, volume 89; *University of Utah Law Review*, number 2020; and *Brigham Young University Law Review*, number 2019; reprinted by permission of the journals.

Mostly, I am thankful to my family: Lloyd, Christine, Bianca, and Joan Bradshaw and Kevin, Carolyn, and James Jerde, and my wonderful extended family including the beloved Fourth of July crew, of whom Niels and Betty Lou Bradshaw and Julia Kardon were tremendously helpful in thinking through this project. Roy and Jean Bradshaw, Dan and Laurel Bringle, Ann-Marie and Ted Merkle, Joe and Sue Rovito, and Jim and Jean Tyhurst have all been special to me since childhood, with a lasting impact that has stayed with me throughout my life. I am also fortunate to have beloved friends who are like family: Robin Anwaya, Jason Bradford, Ellenna Berger, Juliet Burgess, Jennifer Elliott, Sarah Flack, Melissa Kwan, Jessica Monreau, Megan Sable, Annie Shoen, Mary Bruce, the YTT Crew, Koala Moms of Temple Solel, and my Cooking Club. Living with animals has been a remarkable confirmation of their deep capacity; for sharing their lives with me, I am thankful to Sparky, Coal, Tonka, Remington, Meow Mi, and Jackson.

Notes

INTRODUCTION

1. Elizabeth Kolbert, *The Sixth Extinction: An Unnatural History* (New York: Henry Holt, 2014).

2. Edward O. Wilson, *Half Earth: Our Planet's Fight for Life* (New York: Liveright Publishing Corp., 2016).

3. See Karen Bradshaw, "Animal Property Rights," *University of Colorado Law Review* 89 (2018): 830–35.

CHAPTER ONE

1. Richard A. Posner, "Animal Rights," *Yale Law Journal* 110 (2000): 539; Richard Epstein, "Animals as Objects, or Subjects, of Rights" (John M. Olin Program in Law & Economics, Working Paper No. 171, 2002).

2. *Animal Welfare Act, U.S. Code* 7 (2017), §§ 2131–2159. For additional examples of statutes addressing only some members of the animal kingdom, see *Bald and Golden Eagle Protection Act, U.S. Code* 16 (2017), §§ 668–668d; *Wild Free-Roaming Horses and Burros Act, U.S. Code* 16 (2017), §§ 1331–1340; *Marine Mammal Protection Act, U.S. Code* 16 (2017), §§ 1361–1407; *Endangered Species Act, U.S. Code* 16 (2017) §§ 1531–1543.

3. Tom Regan, *The Case for Animal Rights* (Berkeley: University of California Press, 2004).

4. Gary L. Francione, "Animal Rights and Animal Welfare," *Rutgers Law Review* 48 (1996): 398–99. Gary Francione, *The Animal Rights*

Debate: Abolition or Regulation? (New York: Columbia University Press, 2010).

5. David S. Favre, *Respecting Animals: A Balanced Approach to Our Relationship with Pets, Food, and Wildlife* (Amherst, NY: Prometheus, 2018).

6. Justin Marceau, *Beyond Cages: Animal Law and Criminal Punishment* (Cambridge: Cambridge University Press, 2019).

7. *Cetacean Cmty. v. Bush*, 386 F. 3d 1169 (9th Cir. 2004); *Tilikum ex rel. People for the Ethical Treatment of Animals v. Sea World Parks & Entm't Inc.*, 842 F. Supp 2d 1259 (S.D. Cal. 2012). But, see *Palilia v. Haw. Dept. Land & Nat. Res.*, 852 F. 2d 1106, 1107 (9th Cir. 1988). Cass R. Sunstein, "Standing for Animals" (University of Chicago Public Law & Legal Theory Working Paper No. 6, 1999), 3; Cass R. Sunstein, "Standing for Animals (With Notes on Animal Rights)," *UCLA Law Review* 47 (2000): 1333.

8. Annecoos Wiersema, "Incomplete Bans and Uncertain Markets in Wildlife Trade," *University of Pennsylvania Asian Law Review* 12 (2016). Irus Braverman, *Zooland: The Institution of Captivity (The Cultural Lives of Law)* (Stanford: Stanford University Press, 2013), 62. Elizabeth Kolbert, *The Sixth Extinction: An Unnatural History* (New York: Henry Holt, 2014).

9. Christopher Stone, *Should Trees Have Standing? Law, Morality, and the Environment*, 3rd ed. (Oxford: Oxford University Press, 2010).

10. E. L. O'Donnell and J. Talbot-Jones, "Creating Legal Rights for Rivers: Lessons from Australia, New Zealand, and India," *Ecology and Society* 23, no. 1 (2018): 7, https://doi.org/10.5751/ES-09854–230107. Jason Daley, "Toledo, Ohio, Just Granted Lake Erie the Same Legal Rights as People," *Smithsonian.com*, March 1, 2019, https://www .smithsonianmag.com/smart-news/toledo-ohio-just-granted-lake -erie-same-legal-rights-people-180971603/.

11. For a discussion of biocentricity, a worldview which conceives of humans as part of, but not the focus of, the natural environment, see Paul W. Taylor, *Respect for Nature: A Theory of Environmental Ethics* (Princeton, NJ: Princeton University Press, 1986).

12. Several scholars have provided excellent, extended accounts of this discussion. John Locke, *Two Treatises of Government*, edited and with an introduction by Thomas I. Cook (1690; New York: Hafner Press, 1947), 135 ("it is the taking of any party of what is common, and

removing it out of the state nature leaves it in, which begins the property"); Adam Smith, *An Inquiry Into the Nature and Causes of the Wealth of Nations* (1776; London: Electric Book Co., 2001), 73–82 (suggesting that property was not a natural right but instead inexorably intertwined with government); William Blackstone, *Commentaries on the Laws Of England*, facsimile ed. (1765–69; Chicago: University of Chicago Press, 1979), 2 (describing the transfer from unclaimed land into property as a two-step process: prolonged occupancy and investment of labor).

13. Carol M. Rose, "Property as Storytelling: Perspectives from Game Theory, Narrative Theory, Feminist Theory," *Yale Journal of Law and the Humanities* 2 (1990): 37, 51–53. Armen A. Alchain and Harold Demsetz, "The Property Rights Paradigm," *Journal of Economic History* 33 (1973): 16; Terry L. Anderson and P. J. Hill, "The Evolution of Property Rights: A Study of the American West," *Journal of Law and Economics* 18 (1975): 163 ("much less attention been given the question of how the property rights structure comes into being"). Lee Anne Fennell, "The Problem of Resource Access," *Harvard Law Review* 126 (2013): 1471, 1478 ("Coase's framework assumes the existence of property rights.").

14. Harold Demsetz, "Toward a Theory of Property Rights," *American Economic Review* 57, no. 2 (May 1967): 350 (noting that private property emerges when the gains of internalization of externalities exceed the costs of internalization).

15. Following Demsetz, economists Terry Anderson and P. J. Hill noted that the decision to create property rights was essentially determined by the marginal costs and benefits of doing so. They sought to identify the nature of the cost-benefit functions. They tested the theory against property rights governing land, livestock, and water in the western United States. Subsequent economists constructed case studies to describe the land titling process in Brazilian frontiers and American plains. Anderson and Hill, "The Evolution of Property Rights." Richard Epstein provided a hypothetical natural law account. See generally, Epstein, "Animals as Objects."

16. Thomas W. Merrill, "Introduction: The Demsetz Thesis and Evolution of Property Rights," *Journal of Legal Studies* 31 (2002): 331–32.

17. For the history of this scholarship, see, e.g., Thomas W. Merrill, "Property and the Right to Exclude," *Nebraska Law Review* 77 (1998): 730; Thomas W. Merrill, "The Landscape of Constitutional Property,"

Virginia Law Review 86 (2000): 885; Thomas W. Merrill and Henry E. Smith, "The Property/Contract Interface," *Columbia Law Review* 101 (2001): 773; Thomas W. Merrill and Henry E. Smith, "What Happened to Property in Law and Economics?," *Yale Law Journal* 111 (2001): 357; Thomas W. Merrill and Henry E. Smith, "The Morality of Property," *William & Mary Law Review* 48 (2007): 1849; Thomas W. Merrill and Henry E. Smith, "Making Coasean Property More Coasean," *Journal of Law and Economics* 54 (2011): S77; Thomas W. Merrill, "Property as Modularity," *Harvard Law Review Forum* 125 (2012): 151; Thomas W. Merrill, "The Property Strategy," *University of Pennsylvania Law Review* 160 (2012): 2061; Thomas W. Merrill, "Possession as a Natural Right," *New York University Journal of Law & Liberty* 9 (2015): 345; Thomas W. Merrill, "Property and Sovereignty, Information and Audience," *Theoretical Inquires in Law* 18 (2017): 417.

18. Gregory S. Alexander, "The Social-Obligation Norm in American Property Law," *Cornell Law Review* 94 (2009): 745; Eduardo M. Peñalver, "Land Virtues," *Cornell Law Review* 94 (2009): 821; Joseph William Singer, "Democratic Estates: Property Law in a Free and Democratic Society," *Cornell Law Review* 94 (2009): 1009.

19. James Krier, "Evolutionary Theory and the Origin of Property Rights," *Cornell Law Review* 95 (2009): 151 (citing to David Hume, *A Treatise of Human Nature*, edited by L. A. Selby-Bigge, 2nd ed. [1740; Oxford: Oxford University Press, 1978], bk.3, pt.2, §7, at 538); Herbert Gintis, "The Evolution of Private Property," *Journal of Economic Behavior & Organization* 64 (2007): 1, 15.

20. Plato, *Republic of Plato*, trans. and ed. Allan Bloom, 2nd ed. (New York: Basic, 1991).

21. Aristotle, *Rhetoric*, trans. W. Rhys Roberts, ed. Friedrich Solmen (New York: Modern Library, 1984).

22. John Locke, *Two Treatises of Government*, ed. Thomas I. Cook (1690; New York: Hafner Press, 1947).

23. Albert W. Alschuler, "Rediscovering Blackstone," *University of Pennsylvania Law Review* 2 (1996): 145.

24. R. H. Coase, "The Problem of Social Cost," *Journal of Law and Economics* 3 (1960): 1, 44.

25. Hume, *A Treatise of Human Nature*, 489.

26. Henry E. Smith, "Custom in American Property Law: A Vanishing Act," *Texas International Law Journal* 48 (2013): 507, 515.

27. Richard Epstein, "How Spontaneous? How Regulated? The Evolution of Property Rights Systems," *Iowa Law Review* 100 (2015): 2341, 2343–44.

28. Robert C. Ellickson, "Property in Land," *Yale Law Journal* 102 (1993): 1315, 1344.

29. Ellickson, "Property in Land," 1329.

30. Robert C. Ellickson, "The Inevitable Trend Toward Universally Recognizable Signals of Property Claims: An Essay for Carol Rose," *William & Mary Bill of Rights Journal* 19 (2011): 1015, 1029, n. 76; Robert C. Ellickson, "Stone-age Property in Domestic Animals: An Essay for Jim Krier," *Brigham-Kanner Property Rights Conference Journal* 2 (2013): 1.

31. Richard Pipes, *Property and Freedom* (New York: Alfred A. Knopf, 1999), 66–68.

32. Jeffrey Evans Stake, "The Property 'Instinct,'" *Philosophical Transactions of the Royal Society of London B* 359 (2004): 1763, 1767.

33. Krier, "Evolutionary Theory," 139.

34. John Maynard Smith and Geoff A. Parker, "The Logic of Asymmetric Contests," *Animal Behaviour* 24 (1976): 159.

35. Over a thousand papers have empirically tested and expanded upon the model. Susan E. Riechert, "Maynard Smith & Parker's (1976) Rule Book for Animal Contests, Mostly," *Animal Behaviour* 86 (2013): 3, 5.

36. Krier, "Evolutionary Theory," 154 (citing to Robert Sugden, *The Economics of Rights, Co-operation and Welfare* [1986; Palgrave Macmillan, 2004]). William Henry Burt, "Territoriality and Home Range Concepts as Applied to Mammals," *Journal of Mammalogy* 24 (1943): 346, 346.

37. Kathryn Loncarich, "Nature's Law: The Evolution of Property Rights," *Pace Law Review* 35 (2014): 580, 602–13.

38. Jerram L. Brown, "The Evolution of Diversity in Avian Territorial Systems," *Wilson Bulletin* 76, no. 2 (1964): 162.

39. J. P. Myers, P. G. Connors, and F. A. Pitelka, "Territory Size in Wintering Sanderlings: The Effects of Prey Abundance and Intruder Density," *Auk* 96 (1979): 551, 559.

40. Jack da Silva, Rosie Woodroffe, and David W. Macdonald, "Habitat, Food Availability and Group Territoriality in the European Badger, Meles meles," *Oecologia* 95 (1993): 558, 563.

41. Graham H. Pyke, "The Economics of Territory Size and Time Budget in the Golden-Winged Sunbird," *American Naturalist* 114 (1979): 131.

42. John P. Ebersole, "Food Density and Territory Size: An Alternative Model and a Test on the Reef Fish Eupomacentrus Leucostictus," *American Naturalist* 115 (1980): 492, 507, n. 86 at 494.

43. Pyke, "Economics of Territory Size," 139.

44. Scott M. Lanyon and Charles F. Thompson, "Site Fidelity and Habitat Quality as Determinants of Settlement Pattern in Male Painted Buntings," *Condor* 88 (1986): 206, 210, n. 82.

45. Lesley J. Morrell and Hanna Kokko, "Adaptive Strategies of Territory Formation," *Behavioral Ecology and Sociobiology* (2003): 385, 393, n. 141.

46. Burt Hölldobler and Charles J. Lumsden, "Territorial Strategies in Ants," *Science* 210 (1980): 732, n. 143.

47. H. H. Kruuk and T. Parish, "Changes in the Size of Groups and Ranges of the European Badger (Meles meles L.) in an Area in Scotland," *Journal of Animal Ecology* 56 (February 1987): 351, 363.

48. Judy A. Stamps and V. V. Krishnan, "A Learning-Based Model of Territory Establishment," *Quarterly Review of Biology* 74, no. 3 (September 1999): 540.

49. Burt, "Territoriality and Home Range Concepts," 351.

50. J. H. Crook, "The Adaptive Significance of Avian Social Organizations," *Animal Behaviour* 12 (1964): 393, 393.

51. J. H. Crook and J. S. Gartlan, "Evolution of Primate Societies," *Nature* 210 (1996): 1200.

52. D. W. Macdonald and D. D. P. Johnson, "Patchwork Planet: The Resource Dispersion Hypothesis, Society, and the Ecology of Life," *Journal of Zoology* 295 (2015): 75, 76.

53. Macdonald and Johnson, "Patchwork Planet."

54. N. Yamaguchi and D. W. Macdonald, "The Burden of Co-Occupancy: Intraspecific Resource Competition and Spacing Patterns in American Mink, Mustela vison," *Journal of Mammology* 84 (2003): 1341, 1351.

55. Macdonald and Johnson, "Patchwork Planet," 90.

56. Virginia Morell, "Chimpanzees, Bonobos, and Even Humans May Share Ancient Body Language," *Science*, February 27, 2018, http://

www.sciencemag.org/news/2018/02/chimpanzees-bonobos-and-even
-humans-may-share-ancient-body-language.

57. Macdonald and Johnson, "Patchwork Planet," 89–90.

58. Samantha J. Gray, Susanne P. Jensen, and Jane L. Hurst, "Effects
of Resource Distribution on Activity and Territory Defence in House
Mice, Mus Domesticus," *Animal Behaviour* 63 (2002): 531.

59. Dominic D. P. Johnson et al., "Does the Resource Dispersion
Hypothesis Explain Group Living?," *Trends in Ecology & Evolution* 17
(2002): 563, 569.

60. Johnson et al., "Resource Dispersion Hypothesis."

61. Thomas Nagel, "What Is It Like To Be a Bat?," *Philosophical
Review* 83 (1974): 453.

62. Rachel Nussbaum Wichert and Martha C. Nussbaum, "Scientific Whaling? The Scientific Research Exception and the Future of
the International Whaling Commission," *Journal of Human Development and Capabilities* 18, no. 3 (2017): 365–66. Anders Schinkel, "Martha Nussbaum on Animal Rights," *Ethics and the Environment* 13, no. 1
(Spring 2008): 46–48, https://doi.org/10.1353/een.0.0000. Martha
Nussbaum has considered extending the theory of justice to previously
neglected groups, including nonhuman animals. See Martha C. Nussbaum, *Frontiers of Justice: Disability, Nationality, Species Membership*
(Cambridge, MA: Belknap Press of Harvard University Press, 2006).
Rather than only treating animals with compassion and humanity,
Nussbaum develops a theory of animal rights, see Martha C. Nussbaum, "Animal Rights: The Need for a Theoretical Basis," *Harvard
Law Review* 114 (2001): 1548–49 (book review). Her theory includes a
list of animal capabilities analogous to an earlier list of central human
capabilities: "Working With and For Animals: Getting the Theoretical
Framework Right," *Denver Law Review* 94 (2017): 609–25. A longer
version is published in the *Journal of Human Development and Capabilities* (2018). Forthcoming book from Simon and Schuster.

63. Sue Donaldson and Will Kymlicka, *Zoopolis: A Political Theory of
Animal Rights* (Oxford: Oxford University Press, 2011).

64. John Hadley, *Animal Property Rights: A Theory of Habitat Rights
for Wild Animals* (Lanham, MD: Lexington Books, 2015). See also
Steve Cookie, "Animal Kingdoms: On Habitat Rights for Wild Animals," *Environmental Values* 26 (2017): 53. Josh Milburn, "Nonhuman

Animals as Property Holders: An Exploration of the Lockean Labour-Mixing Account," *Environmental Values* 26 (2017): 629.

CHAPTER TWO

1. *Endangered Species Act of 1973, U.S. Code* 16 (2012), §§ 1531–1544; *TVA v. Hill*, 437 U.S. 153 (1978).

2. Barton H. Thompson Jr., "The Endangered Species Act: A Case Study in Takings and Incentives," *Stanford Law Review* 49, no. 49 (1997): 305; Martin B. Main, Fritz M. Roka, and Reed F. Noss, "Evaluating Costs of Conservation," *Conservation Biology* 13, no. 6 (1999): 1265.

3. R. Patrick Rawls and David N. Laband, "A Public Choice Analysis of Endangered Species Listings," *Public Choice* 121, no. 3–4 (December 2004): 263, https://doi.org/10.1007/s11127–004–9784–4; Amy Whritenour Ando, "Waiting to Be Protected Under the Endangered Species Act: The Political Economy of Regulatory Delay," *Journal of Law and Economics* 42 (1999): 30. Daowei Zhang, "Endangered Species and Timber Harvesting: The Case of the Red-Cockaded Woodpeckers," *Economic Inquiry* 42 (2004): 162–63.

4. 93rd Cong., 1st Sess., *Congressional Record* 119 pt. 35: 19138 (1973) (statement of Sen. Williams); 93rd Cong., 1st Sess., *Congressional Record* 119 pt. 35: 30528 (1973); see also 93rd Cong., 1st Sess., *Congressional Record* 119 pt. 35: 25676 (1973); 93rd Cong., 1st Sess., *Congressional Record* 119 pt. 35: 30162 (1973) (Statement of Rep. Sullivan); Thomas F. Darin, "Designating Critical Habitat Under the Endangered Species Act: Habitat Protection Versus Agency Discretion," *Harvard Environmental Law Review* 24 (2000): 213.

5. Challie Facemire and Karen Bradshaw, "Biodiversity Loss Viewed through the Lens of Mismatched Property Rights," *International Journal of the Commons* (forthcoming 2020). Liam Stack, "Wildlife Refuge Occupied in Protest of Oregon Ranchers' Prison Terms," *New York Times*, January 2, 2016, https://www.nytimes.com/2016/01/03/us/oregon-ranchers-will-return-to-prison-angering-far-right-activists.html. Brendon Swedlow, "Scientists, Judges, and Spotted Owls: Policymakers in the Pacific Northwest," *Duke Environmental Law & Policy Forum* 13, no. 2 (Spring 2003): 187. Jonathan Thompson, "The First Sagebrush Rebellion: What Sparked It and How It Ended," *High Country News*, January 14, 2016, https://www.hcn.org/articles/a-look-back-at-the-first-sagebrush-rebellion.

CHAPTER THREE

1. Harold Demsetz, "Toward a Theory of Property Rights," *American Economic Review* 57, no. 2 (May 1967): 347.

2. William H. Burt, "Territoriality and Home Range Concepts as Applied to Mammals," *Journal of Mammalogy* 24, no. 3 (August 1943): 346.

3. Demsetz, "Toward a Theory of Property Rights," 347; Henry E. Smith, "Property as a Law of Things," *Harvard Law Review* 125 (2002): 1629; Thomas W. Merrill and Henry E. Smith, "The Morality of Property," *William & Mary Law Review* 48, no. 5 (2007): 1850.

4. Demsetz, "Toward a Theory of Property Rights," 347.

5. Joseph William Singer, "The Rule of Reason in Property Law," *UC Davis Law Review* 46, no. 5 (June 2013): 1390–1420.

6. Merrill and Smith, "The Morality of Property."

7. Animals may also assert ownership claims over chattel. Sarah F. Brosnan, "Property in Nonhuman Primates," in *Origins of Ownership of Property: New Directions for Child and Adolescent Development*, ed. H. Ross and O. Friedman (San Francisco: Jossey-Bass, 2011), 13.

8. Merrill and Smith, "The Morality of Property." But see Carol M. Rose, "Canons of Property Talk, or, Blackstone's Anxiety," *Yale Law Journal* 108 (1999): 601; Luca Giuggioli, Jonathan R. Potts, and Stephen Harris, "Animal Interactions and the Emergence of Territoriality," *PLoS Computational Biology* 7, no. 3 (March 2011): 1.

9. Graham H. Pyke, Michelle Christy, and Richard E. Major, "Territoriality in Honeyeaters: Reviewing the Concept and Evaluating Available Information," *Australian Journal of Zoology* 44 (1996): 305.

10. Jeff Ollerton and Clive Nuttman, "Aggressive Displacement of Carpenter Bees Xlocopa Nigrita from Flowers of Lagenaria Spaerica (Cuurbitaceae) by Territorial Male Eastern Olive Sunbirds (Cyanomitra Olivacea) in Tanzania," *Journal of Pollination Ecology* 11 (2013): 21.

11. V. Lowell Diller et al., "Demographic Response of Northern Spotted Owls to Barred Owl Removal," *Journal of Wildlife Management* 80 (2016): 691.

12. Pyke, Christy, and Major, "Territoriality in Honeyeaters," 299 ("An individual or group might, for example, be territorial towards conspecifics but not towards other species").

13. Compare Pyke, Christy, and Major, "Territoriality in Honeyeaters," 305, with Elinor Ostrom, *Governing the Commons: The Evolution*

of Institutions for Collective Action (Cambridge: Cambridge University Press, 1990); Bonnie J. McCay and James A. Acheson, *The Question of the Commons: The Culture and Ecology of Communal Resources* (Tucson: University of Arizona Press, 1987).

14. W. Jędrzejewski et al., "Territory Size of Wolves Canis Lupis: Linking Local (Białowieża Primeval Forest, Poland) and Holarctic-Scale Patterns," *Ecography* 30 (2007): 66; Marion Valeix et al., "Influence of Prey Dispersion on Territory and Group Size of African Lions: A Test of the Resource Dispersion Hypothesis," *Ecology* 93 (2012): 2490.

15. Jędrzejewski et al., "Territory Size of Wolves."

16. Pyke, Christy, and Major, "Territoriality in Honeyeaters."

17. H. A. Isack and H. U. Reyer, "Honeyguides and Honey Gatherers: Interspecific Communication in a Symbiotic Relationship," *Science* 243 (1989): 1343.

18. John Robbins, "Paying Farmers to Welcome Birds," *New York Times*, April 14, 2014, https://www.nytimes.com/2014/04/15/science/paying-farmers-to-welcome-birds.html.

19. Leon Marshall, "Wild Dog Urine May Be Used as 'Fences in Africa,'" *National Geographic News*, March 11, 2004.

20. Isack and Reyer, "Honeyguides and Honey Gatherers."

21. Scott M. Lanyon and Charles F. Thompson, "Site Fidelity and Habitat Quality as Determinants of Settlement Pattern in Male Painted Buntings," *Condor* 88 (1986): 210.

22. "Rams, Chargers Ready to Sell Best Seats at New Stadium," *USA Today*, March 7, 2018, https://www.usatoday.com/story/sports/nfl/2018/03/07/rams-chargers-ready-to-sell-best-seats-at-new-stadium/32690479/ (explaining the concept of a "personal seat license," costing individuals upwards of $100,000).

23. Brosnan, "Property in Nonhuman Primates," 13.

24. Demsetz, "Toward a Theory of Property Rights," 350 (noting that private property emerges when the gains of internalization of externalities exceed the costs of internalization).

25 . Richard A. Peters et al., "Social Context Affects Tail Displays by Phrynocephalus vlangalii Lizards from China," *Scientific Reports* 6 (2016): 3 ("[T]he level of territorial behavior exhibited will vary according to the perceived value of the resource"); Lanyon and Thompson, "Site Fidelity and Habitat Quality." But see John P. Ebersole, "Food Density and Territory Size: An Alternative Model and a Test on the

Reef Fish Eupomacentrus Leucostictus," *American Naturalist* 115 (1980): 507.

26. Merrill and Smith, "The Morality of Property."

27. John Locke, *Two Treatises of Government*, ed. Thomas I. Cook (New York: Hafner Press, 1947): 135.

28. Steven Shavell, "Economic Analysis of Property Law," *National Bureau of Economic Research*, Working Paper No. 9695 (May 2003): 8; Robert C. Ellickson, "Property in Land," *Yale Law Journal* 102 (1993): 1344.

29. Merrill and Smith, "The Morality of Property"; Robert C. Ellickson, "The Inevitable Trend toward Universally Recognizable Signals of Property Claims: An Essay for Carol Rose," *William & Mary Bill of Rights Journal* 19 (2011): 1029 n. 76.

30. Compare Lior Jacob Strahilevitz, "The Right to Abandon," *University of Pennsylvania Law Review* 158 (2010): 366, with Brosnan, "Property in Nonhuman Primates."

31. Brosnan, "Property in Nonhuman Primates."

32. Strahilevitz, "The Right to Abandon."

33. Brosnan, "Property in Nonhuman Primates," 14.

34. William Blackstone, *Commentaries on the Laws of England*, facsimile ed. (1765–69; Chicago: University of Chicago Press, 1979), 2.

35. Locke, *Two Treatises of Government*, 135.

36. *Homestead Act of 1962*, Public Law 37–64, *U.S. Statutes at Large* 12: 392.

37. *Dolan v. City of Tigard*, 512 U.S. 374 (1994); *Nollan v. Cal. Coastal Comm'n*, 483 U.S. 825 (1987); *Penn Cent. Transp. Co. v. City of New York*, 438 U.S. 104 (1978).

38. "Prairie Dog, Cynomys Ludovicianus," *National Geographic*, accessed January 15, 2018, http://animals.nationalgeographic.com/animals /mammals/prairie-dog/.

39. Caroline Fraser, "The Crucial Role of Predators: A New Perspective on Ecology," *Yale Environment 360*, September 15, 2011, https:// e360.yale.edu/features/the_crucial_role_of_predators_a_new_per spective_on_ecology.

40. Burt, "Territoriality and Home Range Concepts," 346.

41. Ellickson, "The Inevitable Trend," 1029 n. 76.

42. Carol M. Rose, "Possession as the Origin of Property," *University of Chicago Law Review* 52 (1985): 82.

43. Ellickson, "The Inevitable Trend," 1029–32.

44. Carlos López González and David Brown, *Borderland Jaguars: Tigres de la Frontera* (Salt Lake City: University of Utah Press, 2001).

45. Walter Leuthold, *African Ungulates: A Comparative Review of Their Ethology and Behavioral Ecology* (Berlin: Springer-Verlag, 1977), 34.

46. Robert C. Ellickson, *Order Without Law: How Neighbors Settle Disputes* (Cambridge, MA: Harvard University Press, 1991).

47. Pilar López and José Martín, "Chemical Rival Recognition Decreases Aggression Levels in Male Iberian Wall Lizards, Podarcis hispanica," *Behavioral Ecology and Sociobiology* 51, no. 5 (April 2002): 461.

48. Tristram D. Wyatt, *Pheromones and Animal Behavior: Chemical Signals and Signatures*, 2nd ed. (New York: Cambridge University Press, 2014), 115.

49. Marshall, "Wild Dog Urine."

50. George C. Eickwort and Howard S. Ginsberg, "Foraging and Mating Behavior in Apoidea," *Annual Review of Entomology* 25 (1980): 431.

51. Luis Llaneza, Emilio J. García, and José Vicente López-Bao, "Intensity of Territorial Marking Predicts Wolf Reproduction: Implications for Wolf Monitoring," *PLoS ONE* 9, no. 3 (2014): 2.

52. Wyatt, *Pheromones and Animal Behavior*, 114; Robert F. Noyes et al., "Social Structure of Feral House Mouse (Mus musculus L.) Populations: Effects of Resource Partitioning," *Behavioral Ecology and Sociobiology* 10 (1982): 157.

53. John M. Burt and Michael D. Beecher, "The Social Interaction Role of Song in Song Sparrows: Implications for Signal Design," *Comparative Cognition & Behavior Reviews* 3 (2008): 87; Peter Marler and John G. Vandenbergh, *Social Behavior and Communication: Handbook of Behavioral Neurobiology* (New York: Springer, 1979).

54. Fred H. Harrington, "Aggressive Howling in Wolves," *Animal Behaviour* 35, no. 1 (February 1987): 11, https://doi.org/10.1016/S0003-3472(87)80204-X.

55. Wyatt, *Pheromones and Animal Behavior*, 114; Noyes et al., "Social Structure of Feral House Mouse," 157.

56. Shavell, "Economic Analysis of Property Law," 11.

57. J. Maynard Smith and G. R. Price, "The Logic of Animal Conflict," *Nature* 246 (1973): 15–18 (noting that conflicts between animals of the same species often do not result in serious injury).

58. Wyatt, *Pheromones and Animal Behavior*, 114.

59. Wayne Gard, "Fence Cutting," *Handbook of Texas Online*, uploaded June 12, 2010, http://tshaonline.org/handbook/online/articles/auf01.

60. Wyatt, *Pheromones and Animal Behavior*, 114 (noting that "[a]nimals will go to some risk to investigate and over-mark intruders' scent marks").

61. Ellickson, *Order Without Law*.

62. Mark A. Bee, "A Test of the 'Dear Enemy Effect' in the Strawberry Dart-Poison Frog (Dendrobates pumilio)," *Behavioral Ecology and Sociobiology* 54 (2003): 601.

63. Jaroslav Picman, "Territory Establishment, Size, and Tenacity by Male Red-Wing Blackbirds," *Auk* 104, no. 3 (July 1987): 405.

64. Joseph O'Meara, "Legal Status of the Spite Fence in Ohio," *University of Cincinnati Law Review* 2 (1928): 164.

65. L. K. Yille, "Blood In, Buyout: A Property & Economic Approach to Street Gangs," *Wisconsin Law Review* 102 (2015): 1128.

66. Scott F. Lovell and M. Ross Lein, "Neighbor-stranger Discrimination by Song in a Suboscine Bird, the Alder Flycatcher, *Empidonax alnorum*," *Behavioral Ecology* 15 (2004): 802; López and Martín, "Chemical Rival Recognition."

67. Helga V. Tinnesand et al., "Will Trespassers Be Prosecuted or Assessed According to Their Merits? A Consilient Interpretation of Territoriality in a Group-Living Carnivore, the European Badger (*Meles meles*)," *PLoS ONE* 10 (2015): 7.

68. Michael R. Ross, "Aggression as a Social Mechanism in the Greek Chub (*Semotilus atromaculatus*)," *Copeia* 2 (1977): 395.

69. G. P. Baerends and J. M. Baerends-Van Roon, *An Introduction to the Study of the Ethology of the Cichlid Fishes* (Leiden: E. J. Brill, 1950), 80.

70. Peters et al., "Social Context Affects Tail Displays," 3.

71. Lesley J. Morrell and Hanna Kokko, "Adaptive Strategies of Territory Formation," *Behavioral Ecology and Sociobiology* 54, no. 4 (January 2003): 393.

72. Peters et al., "Social Context Affects Tail Displays," 1.

73. Burt Hölldobler and Charles J. Lumsden, "Territorial Strategies in Ants," *Science* 210, no. 4471 (November 1980): 732.

74. Judy A. Stamps and V. V. Krishnan, "A Learning-Based Model of Territory Establishment," *Quarterly Review of Biology* 74, no. 3 (September 1999): 291.

75. Morrell and Kokko, "Adaptive Strategies of Territory Formation," 393.

76. Catherine Hafer, "On the Origins of Property Rights: Conflict and Production in the State of Nature," *Review of Economic Studies* 73, no. 1 (February 2006): 120.

77. H. H. Kruuk and T. Parish, "Changes in the Size of Groups and Ranges of the European Badger (*Meles meles L*) in an Area in Scotland," *Journal of Animal Ecology* 56 (February 1987): 540; Burt, "Territoriality and Home Range Concepts," 351; J. H. Crook, "The Adaptive Significance of Avian Social Organizations," *Animal Behaviour* 12 (1964): 393; J. H. Crook and J. S. Gartlan, "Evolution of Primate Species," *Nature* 210 (1996): 1200; D. W. Macdonald and D. D. P. Johnson, "Patchwork Planet: The Resource Dispersion Hypothesis, Society, and the Ecology of Life," *Journal of Zoology* 295 (2015): 76.

78. Jeffrey E. Stake, "The Property 'Instinct,'" *Philosophical Transactions of the Royal Society of London B* 359 (2004): 1763.

79. Stake, "The Property 'Instinct.'"

80. López González and Brown, *Borderland Jaguars*.

81. Jan Komdeur and Pim Edelaar, "Evidence that Helping at the Nest Does not Result in Territory Inheritance in the Seychelles Warbler," *Proceedings of the Royal Society of B* 268, no. 1480 (October 2001): 2012.

82. More recently, economist Harold Demsetz suggested that property rights develop in a society when the benefits of having the rights exceeds the costs of creating them. Demsetz, "Toward a Theory of Property Rights," 354.

83. Robert J. Behnke, *Trout and Salmon of North America* (New York: Free Press, 2002), 9.

84. Behnke, *Trout and Salmon*, 28.

85. Hölldobler and Lumsden, "Territorial Strategies in Ants."

86. Andrea Headley and Mohamad G. Alkadry, "The Fight or Flight Response: A Look at Stand Your Ground," *Ralph Bunche Journal of Public Affairs* 5, no. 1 (2016): 1.

87. Stake, "The Property 'Instinct.'"

CHAPTER FOUR

1. James William Gibson, *A Reenchanted World: The Quest for a New Kinship with Nature* (New York: Henry Holt, 2009), 31 (attributing the quote to Massasoit).

2. Peter T. Leeson, "Vermin Trials," *Journal of Law and Economics* 56 (2013): 811.

3. Steven M. Wise, *Rattling the Cage: Toward Legal Rights for Animals* (Cambridge, MA: Perseus Publishing, 2000), 35–36; Charles Siebert, "Should a Chimp Be Able to Sue Its Owner?," *New York Times*, April 23, 2014.

4. Dean Lueck, "Property Rights and the Economic Logic of Wildlife Institutions," *Natural Resources Journal* 35 (1995): 626.

5. "How Long Has the Federal Government Been Setting Aside Lands for Wildlife," National Wildlife Refuge System, U.S. Fish and Wildlife Service, accessed November 5, 2017, https://perma.cc/5Z8Z -VTT8.

6. 1904 N.Y. Laws 1672.

7. 220 N.Y. 423 (1917).

8. See *Gibbs v. Babbitt*, 214 F.3d 483, 496–98 (4th Cir. 2000) (noting that farmers and ranchers take wolves primarily to protect economic assets in the form of livestock and crops). In practice, nongovernmental organizations often compensate livestock losses. Kate Yoshida, "A Symbol of the Range Returns Home," *New York Times*, January 6, 2014, https://perma.cc/AZE3–4K6Z. See *U.S. Code* 16 (2017), § 703.

9. The National Wildlife Refuge System Administration Act of 1966, *U.S. Code* 16 (2017), § 668dd(a)(2).

10. The National Park Service and Related Programs Act, *U.S. Code* 54 (2014), § 100101(a).

11. The Endangered Species Act, *U.S. Code* 16 (2017), § 1531(5).

12. *U.S. Code* 16 (2017), § 1534(a)(1). Fish and Wildlife Act of 1956, *U.S. Code* 16 (2017), §§ 742a–742j; The Fish and Wildlife Coordination Act, *U.S. Code* 16 (2017), §§ 661–667e; The Migratory Bird Conservation Act, *U.S. Code* 16 (2017), §§ 715–715d, 715e, 715f–715k.

13. Karen Bradshaw, "Settling for Natural Resource Damages," *Harvard Environmental Law Review* 40 (2016): 211.

14. U.S. Constitution art. IV, sec. 3, cl. 2.

15. *Kleppe v. New Mexico*, 426 U.S. 529 (1976).

16. *National Audubon Society v. Superior Court*, 33 Cal.3d 419 (Cal. 1983); Cal Water Code § 85086.

17. Karen Bradshaw, "Animal Property Rights," *University of Colorado Law Review* 89 (2018): 809, 828, n. 118 (listing state laws permitting pet trusts).

18. *Naruto v. Slater*, 888 F.3d 418 (9th Cir. 2018). See *Naruto v. Slater*, 2016 WL 362231 (January 28, 2016).

19. Camila Domonoske, "Monkey Can't Own Copyright to His Selfie, Federal Judge Says," *NPR*, January 7, 2016, https://perma.cc/9SAK-FARE.

20. *Naruto*, 888 F.3d at 420.

21. *Cetacean Cmty.*, 386 F.3d at 1169.

CHAPTER FIVE

1. Elinor Ostrom, *Governing the Commons: The Evolution of Institutions for Collective Action* (Cambridge: Cambridge University Press, 1990).

2. See Josh Milburn, "Nonhuman Animals as Property Holders: An Exploration of the Lockean Labour-Mixing Account," *Environmental Values* 26 (2017).

3. See Laurence H. Tribe, "Ten Lessons Our Constitutional Experience Can Teach Us about the Puzzle of Animal Rights: The Work of Steven M. Wise," *Animal Law* 7 (2001): 4.

4. William Jordan, *Divorce Among the Gulls: An Uncommon Look at Human Nature* (North Point, 1991); see also Thomas Nagel, "What Is It Like To Be a Bat?," *Philosophical Review* 83 (1974): 453.

CHAPTER SIX

1. Carol Rose, "The Comedy of the Commons: Custom, Commerce, and Inherently Public Property," *University of Chicago Law Review* 53, no. 3: 740; see also Henry E. Smith, "Community and Custom in Property," *Theoretical Inquiries in Law* 5 (2009): 8; Henry E. Smith, "Custom in American Property Law: A Vanishing Act," *Texas International Law Journal* 48 (2013): 507–9.

2. 71 P.3d 938 (Colo. 2002).

3. Public Access Shoreline Hawaii by Rothstein v. Hawai'i County Planning Commission, 79 Hawai'i 425 (Supreme Court 1995); Article XII, section 7 of the Hawai'i Constitution (1978).

4. 21 U.S. (8 Wheat.) 543 (1823).

5. Richard A. Posner, "Animal Rights," *Yale Law Journal* 110 (2000): 528.

CHAPTER EIGHT

1. Portions of this case study appear in Challie Facemire and Karen Bradshaw, "Biodiversity Loss Viewed through the Lens of Mismatched

Property Rights," *International Journal of the Commons* (forthcoming 2020).

2. George C. Coggins, Charles F. Wilkinson, John D. Leshy, and Robert L. Fischman, *Federal Public Land and Resources Law*, 6th ed., ed. Robert C. Clark et al. (St. Paul: Foundation Press, 2007).

3. K. P. Pitt, "The Wild Free-Roaming Horses and Burros Act: A Western Melodrama," *Environmental Law* 15 (1985): 503, 511.

4. The federal Bureau of Land Management currently charges $2.11 per animal unit month (AUM), compared to an average $20 an AUM on state lands. The Bureau of Land Management and US Forest Service spent a combined $132 million on grazing programs in 2004, but received only $17 million in revenue, operating at a loss of $115 million. Government Accounting Office, *Livestock Grazing: Federal Expenditures and Receipts Vary, Depending on the Agency and the Purpose of the Fee Charged*, September 2005.

5. United States Department of Agriculture, National Agricultural Statistics Service, Grazing Fees: Animal Unit Fee, 17 States (April 2016) available at https://www.nass.usda.gov/Charts_and_Maps/Grazing_Fees/gf_am.php. The cost of private grazing fees is higher still. See Center for Western Priorities, *This Is Why Most Western Ranchers Won't Support States Seizing U.S. Public Lands: Grazing Fees Could Go Up by Orders of Magnitude*, available at: http://westernpriorities.org/2016/02/11/this-is-why-most-western-ranchers-wont-support-states-seizing-u-s-public-lands/ (showing public grazing fees as between $9 and $23 an acre).

6. Federal Land Policy and Management Policy Act of 1976.

7. A. Fuller, "Mustangs: Spirit of the Shrinking West," *National Geographic*, 1997.

8. N. Chokshi, "No, the Federal Government Will Not Kill 45,000 Horses," *New York Times*, September 16, 2016, http://www.nytimes.com/2016/09/16/us/no-the-federal-government-will-not-kill-45000-horses.html.

9. Carlos López González and David Brown, *Borderland Jaguars: Tigres de la Frontera* (Salt Lake City: University of Utah Press, 2001).

10. US Fish and Wildlife Service, US Department of the Interior, *Thick-Billed Parrot (Rhynchopsitta pachyrhyncha) Recovery Plan Addendum* 18 (2013) ("Parrot Recovery Plan").

11. See Alan Lurie and Noel Snyder, "Thick-billed Parrots: Field Observations and History," *Psitta Scene* 13 (2001): 1.

12. WildEarth Guardians, "Fighting for Survival: The Thick-billed Parrot," 1, https://perma.cc/5BN5–2DF5.

13. See Parrot Recovery Plan, 21.

14. Lurie and Snyder, "Thick-billed Parrots," 2; see also Austin Paul Smith, "The Thick-Billed Parrot in Arizona," *Condor* 9 (1907): 104.

15. Lurie and Snyder, "Thick-billed Parrots," 2.

16. Parrot Recovery Plan, 41.

17. See Jones, Comment on *Draft Thick-billed Parrot Recovery Plan*, 44 ("[The] plan seems to be attempting to dodge several issues by emphasizing that the 'primary focus of recovery conservation for the thick-billed parrot must be within Mexico.'").

18. Eva Lee Sargent, Director, Southwest Program, Defenders of Wildlife, Comment on *Draft Thick-billed Parrot Recovery Plan* (2012), 57, https://perma.cc/GDY5–3J2Y ("[S]pecies which are ext[ir]pated can no longer provide these values to the nation.").

19. See Jones, Comment on *Draft Thick-billed Parrot Recovery Plan*, 45 ("Despite the best efforts and commitment of the Mexican government, conservation efforts in the parrots' Mexican range may fail.").

20. See John Fitzgerald and Brett Hartl, Policy Director and Senior Policy Fellow, Society for Conservation Biology, Comment on *Draft Thick-billed Parrot Recovery Plan* (2012), 55, https://perma.cc/GDY5 –3J2Y ("The ability for Thick-billed Parrots to use habitat within the United States is . . . ecologically and biologically important to the recovery of the species.").

21. See Jones, Comment on *Draft Thick-billed Parrot Recovery Plan*, 44–50. But see Gilardi, Comment on *Draft Thick-billed Parrot Recovery Plan*, 51 ("Each one of these [Sky Islands] standing forests is of great cash value, each is prone to serious fire risk (accidental or otherwise), each is used extensively for the production of illegal drugs.").

22. Sartor O. Williams III, Southwest Natural History Institute, Comment on *Draft Thick-billed Parrot Recovery Plan* (2012), 39, https://perma.cc/GDY5–3J2Y ("Those flocks, which were always considered a great novelty, were shot with great gusto, a testament to the mindset of many Americans of the time toward wildlife.").

23. Chris Biro, Founder and Executive Director, Bird Recovery International, Comment on *Draft Thick-billed Parrot Recovery Plan* (2012), 59, https://perma.cc/GDY5–3J2Y ("Mexico has a history of par-

rot smuggling, bribery, and lax enforcement of parrot conservation laws which do not come into play in the United States.").

24. Jones, Comment on *Draft Thick-billed Parrot Recovery Plan*, 44–50 (noting that most of the thick-billed parrot's range in Mexico is already gone while significant portions of Arizona habitat remain in suitable condition).

25. Ruben Marroquin Flores, Mexican Counselor and Sustainability Specialist in Ecological Restoration, Comment on *Draft Thick-billed Parrot Recovery Plan* (2012), 63, https://perma.cc/GDY5-3J2Y.

26. Flores, Comment on *Draft Thick-billed Parrot Recovery Plan*.

27. Flores, Comment on *Draft Thick-billed Parrot Recovery Plan*.

28. Gilardi, Comment on *Draft Thick-billed Parrot Recovery Plan*, 51 (advocating for captive species reintroductions).

29. Luis Fueyo MacDonald, Mexican National Commissioner of Protected Natural Areas, Comment on *Draft Thick-billed Parrot Recovery Plan* (2012), 2, https://perma.cc/GDY5-3J2Y (cautioning that translocation efforts required evaluation of "the success in previous efforts for recovery and translocations, potential habitat at . . . a regional level, connectivity between areas of distribution and [evaluation of] the effectiveness of these measures in terms of cost-benefits for populations.").

30. Fitzgerald and Hartl, Comment on *Draft Thick-billed Parrot Recovery Plan*, 54–56.

31. Biro, Comment on *Draft Thick-billed Parrot Recovery Plan*, 59–62 (noting that the lack of success of the reintroduction was blurred because captive birds were released in close proximity to wild birds).

32. Elizabeth T. Woodin, President, Board Arizona Heritage Alliance, Comment on *Draft Thick-billed Parrot Recovery Plan* (2012), 64, https://perma.cc/GDY5-3J2Y.

33. Fitzgerald and Hartl, Comment on *Draft Thick-billed Parrot Recovery Plan*, 54–56.

34. Biro, Comment on *Draft Thick-billed Parrot Recovery Plan*, 59–62.

35. See Part III.

36. Abigail M. York and Michael L. Schoon, "Collective Action on the Western Range: Coping with External and Internal Threats," *International Journal of the Commons* 5, no. 2 (2011): 389–90 (describing cattle grazing in southern Arizona).

37. York and Schoon, "Collective Action on the Western Range," 394 (noting that cattle grazing interests have over twenty formal organizations to represent their interests across a variety of collaborative environmental issues).

38. Stephen M. Nickelsburg, Note, "Mere Volunteers? The Promise and Limits of Community Based Environmental Protection," *Virginia Law Review* 84, no.7 (October 1998): 1373 (noting that ranchers and the state of Arizona attempted to draft a cooperative agreement that would preempt endangered species act listing of the jaguar). The Fish and Wildlife Service listed the jaguar as an endangered species in 1997. See US Fish and Wildlife Service, Final Rule, "Endangered and Threatened Wildlife and Plants; Final Rule to Extend Endangered Status for the Jaguar in the United States," *Federal Register* 62 (August 21, 1997): 39147 (to be codified at 50 C.F.R. pt. 17).

39. *Arizona Cattle Growers v. Salazar*, 606 F.3d 1160 (9th Cir. 2010). See Jason M. Patlis, "Paying Tribute to Joseph Heller with the Endangered Species Act: When Critical Habitat Isn't," *Stanford Environmental Law Journal* 20 (2001): 137; Daniel J. Rohlf, "Section 4 of the Endangered Species Act: Top Ten Issues for the Next Thirty Years," *Environmental Law* 34 (2004): 547.

40. See Earth First! Jaguar Team, "'Indiana Jones of Wildlife' Joins Ranchers, Mining Executives in Opposing U.S. Jaguar Habitat," Earth First!, February 18, 2013, https://perma.cc/89YH-EFGA (noting designation in 2012 of 838,000 acres of critical habitat for endangered jaguars "caused an uproar from ranchers and mining interests.").

41. See Bradford C. Mank, "Protecting Intrastate Threated Species: Does the Endangered Species Act Encroach on Traditional State Authority and Exceed the Outer Limits of the Commerce Clause?," *Georgia Law Review* 36 (2002): 773–74 (discussing early federal wildlife conservation efforts, including the 1900 Lacey Act and 1918 Migratory Bird Treaty Act).

42. *U.S. Code* 16 (2012) § 1535(a) (requiring Fish and Wildlife Service to "cooperate to the maximum extent practicable with the States.")

43. See Robert L. Fischman and Jaelith Hall-Rivera, "A Lesson for Conservation from Pollution Control Law: Cooperative Federalism for Recovery Under the Endangered Species Act," *Columbia Journal of Environmental Law* 27 (2002): 81; Mank, "Protecting Intrastate Threated Species," 781.

44. Only one commenter identified as being a representative of the villages. See Flores, Comment on *Draft Thick-billed Parrot Recovery Plan*, 63.

45. The Sky Islands region includes lands in southeast Arizona and contains "over half the bird species found in North America and the greatest biological diversity of mammal species north of Mexico." Abigail M. York and Michael L. Schoon, "Collaboration in the Shadow of the Wall: Shifting Power in the Borderlands," *Policy Sciences* 44 (2011): 350.

46. See Julie Ann Gustanki and John B. Wright, "Exploring Net Benefit Maximization: Conservation Easements and the Public-Private Interface," *Law & Contemporary Problems* 74 (2011): 132.

47. Joel Bourne, "El Tigre Comes North," *Audubon*, September 19, 1997, 88. See also Arizona Department of Environmental Quality, "Arizona-Sonora Environmental Strategic Plan 2017–2021," 32.

48. See Hannah Drier, "Desert Tortoise Faces Threat from Its Own Refuge," *Desert News*, August 25, 2013, https://perma.cc/4HLU-5A3Q. See, e.g., Jill S. Heaton et al., "Spatially Explicit Decision Support for Selecting Translocation Areas for Mojave Desert Tortoises," *Biodiversity Conservation* 17 (2008): 580. See also US Fish and Wildlife Serv., "Chapter 7. Guidelines for Handling Desert Tortoises—Mojave Population and Their Eggs," December 2009, 1, https://perma.cc/T4 W7-JYA3.

49. Kurt Repansheck, "Alaska Fish and Game Employees Kill Entire Yukon-Charley Rivers National Preserve Wolf Pack," *National Parks Traveler*, February 28, 2014, https://perma.cc/2U5B-KTQE.

50. See Karen Bradshaw, "Agency Coordination of Private Action: The Role of Relational Contracting," *Texas A&M Law Review* 6 (2018): 229, 257.

51. This case study appears in Karen Bradshaw, *Stakeholder Collaborations for Managing Land and Natural Resources*, Administrative Conference of the United States, Office of the President Report (2018). See acknowledgments for a list of journals in which portions of this book appeared.

52. Western Arctic Caribou Herd Working Group, *Western Arctic Caribou Herd Cooperative Management Plan* (December 2011), 4, http://www.adfg.alaska.gov/static/research/plans/pdfs/wah_management _plan_final_2011.pdf.

53. Interview 1 in Bradshaw, *Stakeholder Collaborations*, 83.

54. Western Arctic Caribou Herd Working Group, *Western Arctic Caribou Herd Cooperative Management Plan*, 6.

55. Interview 16 in Bradshaw, *Stakeholder Collaborations*; see also Ray Barnhardt and Angayuqaq Oscar Kawagley, "Indigenous Knowledge Systems and Alaska Native Ways of Knowing," *Anthropology & Education Quarterly* 36 (2005): 8–9.

56. Denali Daniels and Associates, Inc., "National Strategy on the Arctic Region (NSAR)—Ten Year Renewable Energy Strategy," US Department of Energy, 17, https://www.energy.gov/sites/prod/files/2015/02/f19/NSAR%20Renewable%20Energy%20Meeting%20Notes%20and%20Analysis_Fall%202014.pdf.

57. Mallory Simon, "In Rural Alaska Villages, Families Struggle to Survive," CNN, last updated February 9, 2017, 8:43 p.m., http://www.cnn.com/2009/US/02/09/rural.alaska.villages/index.html.

58. Simon, "In Rural Alaska Villages."

59. Simon, "In Rural Alaska Villages."

60. "National Strategy on the Arctic Region (NSAR)," 52, 57 ("Fuel delivery scares have occurred, related to weather forcing the barge to be delayed or rerouted.").

61. "National Strategy on the Arctic Region (NSAR)," 31 ("Food security is a concern as stores are stocking less food and costs are increasing.").

62. Interview 1 in Bradshaw, *Stakeholder Collaborations*.

63. Jim Dau, Wildlife Biologist for Alaska Department of Fish and Game (ret.), telephone interview, July 25, 2017.

64. Dau, telephone interview.

65. Dau, telephone interview.

66. Western Arctic Caribou Herd Working Group, *Western Arctic Caribou Herd Cooperative Management Plan*, 6.

67. "About," Western Arctic Caribou Herd Working Group, accessed July 21, 2017, https://westernarcticcaribou.net/.

68. "About," Western Arctic Caribou Herd Working Group, accessed July 21, 2017, https://westernarcticcaribou.net/.

69. Dau, telephone interview.

70. "About," Western Arctic Caribou Herd Working Group, 4–5.

71. Joanna Klein, "Protected Wolves in Alaska Face Peril from Beyond Their Preserve," *New York Times*, July 14, 2017, https://www.ny

times.com/2017/07/14/science/wolves-alaska-yukon-charley-pre
serve.html.

CHAPTER NINE

1. Charles Siebert, "Should a Chimp Be Able to Sue Its Owner?,"
New York Times, April 23, 2014; Bruce A. Wagman, Sonia Waisman,
and Pamela D. Frasch, *Animal Law: Cases and Materials* (Durham,
NC: Carolina Academic Press, 2019).

2. *Georgia v. Tenn. Copper Co.*, 237 U.S. 474 (1915); *Missouri v. Illinois*,
200 U.S. 496 (1906).

3. *Clean Air Act, U.S. Code* 42 (1970), §§ 7401–7617; *Clean Water Act,
U.S. Code* 33 (1972), §§ 1251–1388.

4. Jody Freeman and David B. Spence, "Old Statutes, New Problems," *University of Pennsylvania Law Review* 163 (2014): 1.

5. See Jeremy Bentham, *The Theory of Legislation*, ed. C. K. Ogden,
trans. Richard Hildreth (London: Kegan Paul, 1908), 119–20.

6. George C. Coggins, Charles F. Wilkinson, John D. Leshy, and
Robert L. Fischman, *Federal Public Land and Resources Law*, 6th ed.,
ed. Robert C. Clark et al. (St. Paul: Foundation Press, 2007).

7. US Constitution amend. XIX; US Constitution amend. XIV.

8. Karen Bradshaw Schulz and Dean Lueck, "Contracting for Control of Landscape-Level Resources," *Iowa Law Review* 100 (2015): 2507.

9. For a discussion of fish in a stream, suing water polluters, see
Daniel H. Cole, *Pollution & Property: Comparing Ownership Institu-
tions for Environmental Protection* (Cambridge: Cambridge University
Press, 2002).

10. See, e.g., Terry L. Anderson and Hannah Downey, Opinion, "Hunting Can be Good for Lions and Elephants: A Government Report Makes
the Case for Easing the Ban on Importation of Big-game Trophies,"
Wall Street Journal, November 28, 2017, https://perma.cc/ZB28-RCA8;
Manny Fernandez, "Blood and Beauty on a Texas Exotic-Game Ranch,"
New York Times, October 19, 2017, https://www.nytimes.com/2017/10
/19/us/exotic-hunting-texas-ranch.html. For a different perspective on
the relationship between trophy hunting and conservation, see Stephen
Leahy, "Trophy Hunting May Drive Extinctions, Due to Climate
Change," *National Geographic*, November 28, 2017, https://news.national
geographic.com/2017/11/wildlife-watch-trophy-hunting-extinctions
-evolution/.

11. See, e.g., *TVA v. Hill*, 437 U.S. 153 (1978).

12. See, e.g., Joshua Rottman, "Breaking Down Biocentrism: Two Distinct Forms of Moral Concern for Nature," *Frontiers in Psychology* 5 (August 2014): 1.

13. See generally Martin H. Krieger, "What's Wrong with Plastic Trees? Rationales for Preserving Rare Natural Environments Involve Economic, Societal, and Political Factors," *Science* 179, no. 4072 (February 1973): 446.

14. See Cass R. Sunstein, "Incommensurability and Valuation in Law," *Michigan Law Review* 92 (1994): 786.

15. Sunstein, "Incommensurability and Valuation in Law."

16. Richard A. Posner, "Animal Rights," *Yale Law Journal* 110 (2000): 536.

17. Anthony Downs, *Inside Bureaucracy* (Waveland, 1967), 421.

18. Jedediah Purdy, "Coming into the Anthropocene," *Harvard Law Review* 129 (2016): 1635–36 (reviewing Jonathan Z. Cannon, *Environment in the Balance: The Green Movement and the Supreme Court* [Cambridge, MA: Harvard University Press, 2015]).

CHAPTER TEN

1. Christian Walloth, *Emergent Nested Systems: A Theory of Understanding and Influencing Complex Systems as well as Case Studies in Urban Systems* (Springer, 2016).

2. James M. Acheson, *The Lobster Gangs of Maine* (Hanover: University Press of New England, 1988).

3. Robert C. Ellickson, "A Hypothesis of Wealth-Maximizing Norms: Evidence from the Whaling Industry," *Journal of Law, Economics, and Organization* 5 (1989): 83.

4. Harold Demsetz, "Toward a Theory of Property Rights," *American Economic Review* 57, no. 2 (May 1967):

5. Eric A. Feldman, "The Tuna Court: Law and Norms in the World's Premier Fish Market," *California Law Review* 93 (2006): 313, 313–14.

6. Robert C. Ellickson, *Order without Law: How Neighbors Settle Disputes* (Cambridge, MA: Harvard University Press, 1991).

7. "Private Commercial Law in the Cotton Industry: Creating Cooperation Through Rules, Norms, and Institutions," *Michigan Law Review* 99 (2001): 1724; Lisa Bernstein, "Opting Out of the Legal System:

Extralegal Contractual Relations in the Diamond Industry," *Journal of Legal Studies* 21 (1992): 115, 138–43.

8. Terry L. Anderson and P. J. Hill, "The Evolution of Property Rights: A Study of the American West," *Journal of Law and Economics* 18 (1975).

9. For the history of this scholarship, see, e.g., Thomas W. Merrill, "Property and the Right to Exclude," *Nebraska Law Review* 77 (1998): 730; Thomas W. Merrill, "The Landscape of Constitutional Property," *Virginia Law Review* 86 (2000): 885; Thomas W. Merrill and Henry E. Smith, "The Property/Contract Interface," *Columbia Law Review* 101 (2001): 773; Thomas W. Merrill and Henry E. Smith, "What Happened to Property in Law and Economics?," *Yale Law Journal* 111 (2001): 357; Thomas W. Merrill and Henry E. Smith, "The Morality of Property," *William & Mary Law Review* 48 (2007): 1849; Thomas W. Merrill and Henry E. Smith, "Making Coasean Property More Coasean," *Journal of Law and Economics* 54 (2011): S77; Thomas W. Merrill, "Property as Modularity," *Harvard Law Review Forum* 125 (2012): 151; Thomas W. Merrill, "The Property Strategy," *University of Pennsylvania Law Review* 160 (2012): 2061; Thomas W. Merrill, "Possession as a Natural Right," *New York University Journal of Law & Liberty* 9 (2015): 345; Thomas W. Merrill, "Property and Sovereignty, Information and Audience," *Theoretical Inquires in Law* 18 (2017): 417.

10. Gregory S. Alexander, "The Social-Obligation Norm in American Property Law," *Cornell Law Review* 94 (2009): 745; Eduardo M. Peñalver, "Land Virtues," *Cornell Law Review* 94 (2009): 821; Joseph William Singer, "The Rule of Reason in Property Law," *UC Davis Law Review* 46, no. 5 (June 2013).

11. Marion Valeix, Andrew J. Loveridge, and David W. Macdonald, "Influence of Prey Dispersion on Territory and Group Size of African Lions: A Test of the Resource Distribution Hypothesis," *Ecology* 93 (2012): 2490, 2494.

12. Carlos López González and David Brown, *Borderland Jaguars: Tigres de la Frontera* (Salt Lake City: University of Utah Press, 2001), n. 107.

13. Alaskan Eskimo Whaling Commission, Report, *Description of Alaskan Eskimo Bowhead Whale Subsistence Sharing Practices: Including an Overview of Bowhead Whale Harvesting and Community-Based Need* (May 23, 2018), http://www.north-slope.org/assets/images/uploads/Braund _AEWC16_Bowhead_Sharing_Report_5–23–18.pdf.

14. Alaskan Eskimo Whaling Commission, Report, *Description of Alaskan Eskimo Bowhead Whale Subsistence Sharing Practices*, 11.

15. Julie Johnson, *History of Quilting*, last visited January 31, 2019, https://www.emporia.edu/cgps/tales/quilte~1.html.

16. Carl Shapiro, "Navigating the Patent Thicket: Cross Licenses, Patent Pools, and Standard Setting," *Innovation Policy and the Economy* 1 (2000): 119.

17. Albert Einstein: "Bear in mind that the wonderful things you learn in your schools are the work of many generations, produced by enthusiastic effort and infinite labor in every country of the world . . . we mortals achieve immortality in the permanent things which we create in common"; Murray J. Leaf, *An Anthropology of Academic Governance and Institutional Democracy: The Community of Scholars in America* (Palgrave Macmillan, 2019).

CONCLUSION

1. Gregory J. Velicer and Michiel Vos, "Sociobiology of the Myxobacteria," *Annual Review of Microbiology* 63 (2009): 599; Stuart A. West et al., "The Social Lives of Microbes," *Annual Review of Ecology, Evolution, & Systematics* 38 (2007): 53; Christopher J. Marx, "Getting in Touch with Your Friends," *Science* 324 (2009): 1150.

2. See H. J. Schenk et al., "Spatial Root Segregation: Are Plants Territorial," *Advances in Ecological Research* 28 (1999): 146.

3. See Schenk et al., citing Cornelius H. Muller, U.S.D.A. Technical Bulletin No. 923, *Root Development and Ecological Relations of Guayule* (December 1946): 98.

4. "Plant Territoriality," *Science Watch*, March 23, 1993, http://www.nytimes.com/1993/03/23/science/science-watch-plant-territoriality.html.

5. Karine A. Gibbs and Peter Greenberg, "Territoriality in Proteus: Advertisement and Aggression," *Chemical Reviews* 111, no. 1 (2011): 188 (citing R. J. Wolfe, *Journal of Microbiology and Biology Education* 14 [2009]: 6 [http://archive.microbeHbrary.org/edzine/details.asp?id=2jys]).

6. Gibbs and Greenberg, "Territoriality in Proteus."

7. Gibbs and Greenberg, "Territoriality in Proteus," 191.

8. Gibbs and Greenberg, "Territoriality in Proteus," 191.

9. S. K. Aoki, R. Pamma, A. D. Hernday, J. E. Bickham, B. A. Braaten, "Contact Dependent Inhibition of Growth in *Escherichia coli*," *Science* 309 (2005): 1245; M. Vos, G. J. Velicer, "Social Conflict in

Centimeter- and Global-Scale Populations of the Bacterium *Myxococ-cus xanthus*," *Current Biology* 19 (2009): 1763.

10. Gibbs and Greenberg, "Territoriality in Proteus," 189.

11. Gibbs and Greenberg, "Territoriality in Proteus," 189.

12. David L. Chandler, "Tiny Bacterium Provides Window into Whole Ecosystems," *MIT News*, March 27, 2017, http://oceans.mit .edu/news/featured-stories/tiny-bacterium-provides-window-into -whole-ecosystems; R. Braakman, M. J. Follows, and S. W. Chisholm, "Metabolic evolution and the self-organization of ecosystems," *Proceedings of the National Academy of Sciences USA* 114 (April 2017): E3091, https://doi.org/10.1073/pnas.1619573114.

13. Steve Pavlik, *The Navajo and the Animal People: Native American Traditional Ecological Knowledge and Ethnozoology* (Golden, CO: Fulcrum Publishing, 2014) (quoting Navajo Nation Constitution).

14. Mari Margil, "Press Release: Ho-Chunk National General Council Approves Rights of Nature Constitutional Amendment," Community Environmental Legal Defense Fund, September 17, 2018, https:// celdf.org/2018/09/press-release-ho-chunk-nation-general-council -approves-rights-of-nature-constitutional-amendment/.

15. Richard Epstein, "Animals as Objects, or Subjects, of Rights" (John M. Olin Program in Law & Economics, Working Paper No. 171, 2002), 21, 25–26 (advocating for greater protection being afforded to animals "higher on the tree of life").

16. Christopher D. Stone, "Should Trees Have Standing?—Toward Legal Rights for Natural Objects," *Southern California Law Review* 45 (1972): 450.

17. *National Park Service Organic Act*, Public Law 64–235, *U.S. Statutes at Large* 39 (1916): 535.

18. Anti-Defamation League, "Lewis and Clark: The Unheard Voices," *Curriculum Connections* (Fall 2014): 46 https://perma.cc/SPS5-BBV7 (quote attributed to Massasoit).

Index

124, 135; ranchers and, 134; ranges
and, 129; resources and, 126, 128–
31; sanctuaries and, 40, 57, 130;
statutory approach and, 127, 133,
135; wolves and, 125
biofences, 47
biological paradigm: cost-benefit
analysis and, 24–28; environmental issues and, 31; hunting and,
28; literature on, 22–29; migration
and, 25; moral issues and, 29–31;
ownership and, 26; predators and,
25, 28; ranges and, 25–26; resource
distribution hypothesis (RDH)
and, 27–28; territory and, 23–28
birds: Animal Welfare Act and, 12;
behavioral training and, 105;
biodiversity preservation and, 135;
blackbirds, 52, 71, 135; condors, 57;
counts of, 69; doves, 24; eagles,
12, 57, 59; habitat corridors and,
47; hawks, 24; honeyguides, 47;
hunting regulations and, 105;
migration and, 25, 47, 57, 59, 91;
Migratory Bird Conservation Act
and, 59; Migratory Bird Treaty
Act and, 59; parrots and, 7 (*see also*
parrots); Pelican Island Migratory Bird Reservation and, 57;
property law and, 23, 47, 52–54,
56; property theory and, 141, 143;
raising wild, 96; rights of nature
and, 156; Seychelles warblers, 54;
sunbirds, 47; territory and, 25–27,
52–54, 103; trusts and, 69, 71, 135;
vocalizations and, 53
bison, 68
blackbirds, 52, 71, 135
Blackstone, William, 20, 22, 48–49
bobcats, 33
bonobos, 28
Boran people, 47

boundaries, 23, 50–51, 72, 107, 152
Boyd, David, 18, 154–55
Brazil, 17
British Petroleum, 85
Brown, Jerram, 24–25
Buffet, Warren, 92–93
Bureau of Land Management
(BLM), 58, 97–100, 128, 177n4
burros, 12, 98
burrows, 49
butterflies, 53

cages, 4, 13, 132
California, 17, 47, 60, 91, 150
Callaway, R. M., 150
captivity: animal law and, 12–13, 15;
biodiversity loss and, 39; births
in, 96; breeding in, 68, 103–4, 107;
cages and, 4, 13, 132; horses and,
100; lawsuits and, 132; parrots and,
102–4; tortoises and, 107; trusts
and, 68; zoos and, 15, 30, 39, 102,
130
caribou: Alaska and, 7, 95–96, 108–18;
competition and, 126; Congress
and, 112; conservation and, 112,
114–15, 118; ecosystems and, 115,
119; ethics and, 110; food and,
109–11, 119; hunting and, 38,
109–10, 112, 115–16, 118; land use
and, 109; management of, 108–19;
migration and, 108, 110, 117; Native Americans and, 95–96, 109–
14, 117–18; predators and, 38, 116;
private land and, 109, 114; public
land and, 115; ranges and, 108, 115,
117; sociobiological backdrop for,
109–11; stakeholder collaboration
and, 95, 113–18; statutory approach
and, 108, 119; WACHWG and,
112–17; Western Arctic Caribou
Herd and, 108–18; wolves and, 38

www.ingramcontent.com/pod-product-compliance
Lightning Source LLC
Chambersburg PA
CBHW021904020426
42334CB00013B/467